# ASSESSMENT OF COVID-19 RESPONSE IN THE REPUBLIC OF KOREA

APRIL 2021

ADB

ASIAN DEVELOPMENT BANK

© 2021 Asian Development Bank
6 ADB Avenue, Mandaluyong City, 1550 Metro Manila, Philippines
Tel +63 2 8632 4444; Fax +63 2 8636 2444
www.adb.org

Some rights reserved. Published in 2021.

ISBN 978-92-9262-791-1 (print); 978-92-9262-792-8 (electronic); 978-92-9262-793-5 (ebook)
Publication Stock No. TCS210133-2
DOI: http://dx.doi.org/10.22617/TCS210133-2

The views expressed in this publication are those of the authors and do not necessarily reflect the views and policies of the Asian Development Bank (ADB) or its Board of Governors or the governments they represent.

ADB does not guarantee the accuracy of the data included in this publication and accepts no responsibility for any consequence of their use. The mention of specific companies or products of manufacturers does not imply that they are endorsed or recommended by ADB in preference to others of a similar nature that are not mentioned.

By making any designation of or reference to a particular territory or geographic area, or by using the term "country" in this document, ADB does not intend to make any judgments as to the legal or other status of any territory or area.

Corrigenda to ADB publications may be found at http://www.adb.org/publications/corrigenda.

Notes:
In this publication, "$" refers to United States dollars and "W" refers to Korean won.
ADB recognizes "Korea" and "South Korea" as the Republic of Korea.

Cover design by Mike Cortes.

# Contents

# Tables, Figures, and Boxes

**Boxes**

# Foreword

The coronavirus disease (COVID-19) has upended our interconnected world, magnified existing inequalities, and worsened socioeconomic tension. To respond to the unprecedented impacts of the coronavirus, we must understand that pandemics are inherently global issues. The pandemic has made clear our interconnected nature and shown that no country, regardless of its size, wealth, or technological sophistication, can tackle the issue alone. Cooperation and solidarity, partnership, and global governance, including the strong leadership of the United Nations and the World Health Organization, are needed in our fight against COVID-19.

Countries learning from each other is fundamental to overcome the crisis. Listening to scientists and experts and sharing experience and expertise allow effective policies and best practices to be disseminated globally. Advanced information and communication technology is an excellent means of delivering information quickly, and the establishment of a new global information technology–based response platform would allow vetted scientific information and sustainable policy options for dealing with COVID-19 to be rapidly accessible to all countries.

The Republic of Korea (ROK) has received recognition worldwide for its effective response to the coronavirus. This report provides an assessment of the ROK's response to COVID-19, outlining significant factors of its successful response, such as its 3T approach of Testing, Tracing, and Treatment, as well as its economic and social responses. The lessons learned from the case of the ROK can provide important insights for other governments and societies in their efforts to deal with the coronavirus and its societal aftershocks.

While the COVID-19 pandemic has caused untold devastation around the world, it also provides us with a generational opportunity to build back better. We must strengthen our health systems and reduce inequalities to tackle COVID-19, to be prepared for future pandemics and build a better future for all. Every country must recognize that the only way to achieve these objectives is through effective multilateralism and regional cooperation, which is ultimately in everyone's interest. The international community must elevate its collective efforts to address this crisis and develop its information-sharing capacities. Information and knowledge sharing are public goods. Ultimately, the lessons learned from the pandemic must reinvigorate the necessity of cooperation and solidarity based on multilateralism and guide us to a more inclusive, sustainable, and resilient future.

**Ban Ki-moon**
The 8th Secretary General of the United Nations
Chairman of the Ban Ki-moon Foundation for a Better Future

# Acknowledgments

This knowledge product, *Assessment of COVID-19 Response in the Republic of Korea*, has been developed by the Asian Development Bank (ADB) in partnership with the Ban Ki-moon Foundation for a Better Future (BKMF).

ADB and BKMF would like to thank everyone who contributed to the creation of this report and specifically from BKMF: former Ambassador Sook Kim, executive director; Byung-yong Lee, head of planning and policy; former Ambassador Choi, Sung-joo, head of international cooperation; Pak, Yil-ho, head of administration; Tae Yong Jung, director of sustainable development program, who provided overall direction for the report; and Jongwoo Moon, manager.

The expert group of BKMF, led by former ambassador Rae Kwon Chung, supported the technical research. Jae Wook Choi and Chang Soo Kim, medical experts, provided their clinical experience in the field. Valuable inputs from Sung Jin Kang, economist; Zoonky Lee, IT specialist; Woojin Kim, medical expert; Jaewan Kim, sustainable development expert; and research assistants Hyerim Yoo and Hyung Rok Oh, enriched the report.

From ADB, the knowledge product was managed by Susann Roth, advisor and chief of Knowledge Advisory Services Center, Sustainable Development and Climate Change Department (SDCC-KC); and Josephine Jacinto-Aquino, associate knowledge sharing and services officer, SDCC-KC. Miko Mojica, knowledge sharing and services analyst, SDCC-KC, provided support to the production process with the contribution of ADB publishing counterparts and service providers in the Department of Communications including Wickie Mercado, copyeditor; Edith Creus, typesetter; Rodel Bautista, publishing coordinator; Noren Jose, editor; Cynthia Hidalgo, publishing officer; Anthony Victoria, graphic design coordinator; Mike Cortes, cover designer; Lawrence Casiraya, proofreader; and Maricelle Abellar, page proof checker. The report benefitted from the review from Patrick Osewe, chief, health sector group, SDCC; and Robert Guild, chief sector officer, SDCC.

# Abbreviations

| | | |
|---|---|---|
| ADB | – | Asian Development Bank |
| API | – | application open interface |
| COVID-19 | – | coronavirus disease |
| DUR | – | Drug Utilization Review |
| EBS | – | Educational Broadcast System |
| EUA | – | Emergency Use Authorization |
| FDA | – | Food and Drug Administration |
| HIRA | – | Health Insurance Review and Assessment Service |
| IT | – | information technology |
| ICT | – | information and communication technology |
| ITS | – | International Traveler Information System |
| KCDC | – | Korea Centers for Disease Control and Prevention |
| KDI | – | Korea Development Institute |
| KERIS | – | Korea Education and Research Information Service |
| LMS | – | Learning Management System |
| MERS | – | Middle East respiratory syndrome |
| MOE | – | Ministry of Education |
| MOHW | – | Ministry of Health and Welfare |
| MSIT | – | Ministry of Science and ICT |
| OECD | – | Organisation for Economic Co-operation and Development |

| | | |
|---|---|---|
| PPP | – | public–private partnership |
| PUI | – | patient under investigation |
| R&D | – | research and development |
| ROK | – | Republic of Korea |
| RT-PCR | – | real-time polymerase chain reaction |
| SARS | – | severe acute respiratory syndrome |
| SMS | – | Smart Management System |

# 1 Introduction

The coronavirus disease (COVID-19) pandemic is an unprecedented global crisis. Key risks that contributed to this crisis come from the uncertainty of how complex systems react and interact. This includes health, environmental, economic, and political sectors. This exceptional global crisis demands the establishment of a new global governance and a crisis management response approach that is consistent with hyperconnected modern societies. Global hyperconnectivity, powered by information communication technology (ICT) and social media, has proven to be a double-edged sword. On the one hand it could stabilize global response to pandemic by disseminating scientifically solid information, but on the other hand, it could easily destabilize and devastate the painstaking efforts to cope with the pandemic by spreading out false rumors and amplifying fake news instantly around the world. Therefore, the decision-making process for COVID-19 response should be based on science and fast-evolving research with optimal information technology (IT) platform connectivity. This will prevent and minimize the destabilizing effects of false information and maximize the positive impact of an IT platform by offering best available scientifically proven and solid information to the people, policy makers, and medical professionals dealing with the pandemic. Failure to respond appropriately in the initial stage in many countries increased the uncertainty and confusion about the pandemic and unnecessarily politicized the local and global response. This resulted in the collapse of global partnership and systematic management of the pandemic. Under extreme panic triggered by uncertainty, people easily fell into herd mentality and local, national, and global governance for scientific management of pandemic could not function in the way they are supposed to.

The establishment of an IT platform that could deliver vetted, scientific information for rapid response to the pandemic and policy options for sustainable public health management could be a powerful strategy to deal with current and future pandemics and ensures adequate health solutions. The platform will formalize data and information sharing among expert groups and help foster science-based decision-making. When advanced ICT is combined with the platform operation, we can expect an effective response to the global crisis. As the first step to develop the platform ideas, we conducted a case study of how the Republic of Korea (ROK) managed the COVID-19 pandemic.

Management of the COVID-19 pandemic in the ROK has been recognized for its effective outcome without resorting to strict border control and lockdown of its own citizens. The Korean case has been studied as one of the potential models for successful response to the COVID-19 pandemic. The ROK has maintained a high level of transparency and openness in managing the pandemic and presented a unique example of applying advanced science and ICT in maximizing the efficiency of coping with the crisis. In this report, first, we investigate the outbreak of COVID-19 followed by the governance structure to cope with the pandemic situation in the ROK. While in some countries the breach of privacy during the tracing process stirred up sensitive controversies, personal information of confirmed individuals in the ROK have been strictly protected by data privacy and security legislation already in place. In the later chapters, four main significant factors of COVID-19 response—Testing, Tracing, Treatment, and Transparency—are examined thoroughly by demonstrating detailed examples. In the following chapter, economic and social responses to COVID-19 are studied to understand how the ROK has strived to stimulate its stagnant economy, as well as mobilize people to adhere to social distancing.

## Box 1: Timeline of the Coronavirus Disease Infections in the Republic of Korea

The first domestic confirmed case of the coronavirus disease (COVID-19) was identified in the Republic of Korea on 20 January 2020. By 16 February, 30 new confirmed cases due to foreign inflows or local community transmission had been identified, the route of infection was not traceable for all these cases.

On 17 February, the 31st confirmed person (later named as a "super-communicator") was diagnosed in Daegu City. A full-scale epidemiological investigation started for the believers of a religious sect in Daegu where the super-communicator belonged to. Multiple confirmed cases related to super-communicator, and first death occurred in 20 February. The number of confirmed cases continued to increase thereafter, resulting in up to 1,062 cases per day (2 March).

On 6 April, although the number of new confirmed cases decreased to fewer than 50 (47) per day, many cases of group infection occurred mainly in entertainment facilities during the holiday season starting on 30 April.

On 12 August, as a confirmed case occurred in a church in Seoul, the number of related confirmed patients, including visitors, prayers, and family members of the churchgoers, increased to about 200 in 4 days. As a large number of confirmed patients occurred in the greater metropolitan area of Seoul, the government upgraded social distancing level to the second stage only in the capital area, but the number of confirmed cases per day remained in the hundreds.

On 20 September, the number of new confirmed cases per day again declined to fewer than 100 people, and showed a decreasing trend compared to August. However, because of concerns that the number of confirmed cases may increase again starting from the major holiday (Thanksgiving Day) scheduled from 30 September to 4 October, the disease control authorities monitored the trend without lowering the level of quarantine stage.

- First confirmation: 20 January 2020
- Cumulative confirmation: 23,611 (as of 27 September 2020)
- Cumulative deaths: 401 (as of 27 September 2020)
- Fatality rate: 1.70% (as of 27 September 2020)

Source: Government of the Republic of Korea, Ministry of Health and Welfare. Coronavirus Disease-19, Republic of Korea. http://ncov.mohw.go.kr/.

# 2 Governance

## 2.1 National Infectious Disease Crisis Response System

**KEY MESSAGE**

*The Government of the Republic of Korea (ROK) established the relevant laws and basic plans for infectious disease control and prevention based on its experience with epidemics. This enabled systematic quarantine activities of the national and local governments and strengthened them by presenting the basic goals and direction of implementation of infectious disease prevention management. In addition, the Government of the ROK has created a standard manual for risk management that can respond to an outbreak of an infectious disease. This manual was prepared to suggest a pan-governmental crisis management system and direction of activities for each institution.*

The ROK has experienced several cases of public health crises caused by infectious diseases from overseas including the epidemics of severe acute respiratory syndrome (SARS) in 2003, swine flu in 2009, and Middle East respiratory syndrome (MERS) in 2015. Based on these experiences, the Government of the ROK enacted the Infectious Disease Control and Prevention Act (Enforcing Decrees of Infectious Case Control and Prevention was first established as a subordinate statute on 18 January 2010), mandating the Minister of Health and Welfare to establish a comprehensive and systematic basic plan for infectious disease control and prevention every 5 years. On the basis of the basic plan, the head of each local government established and implemented an enforcement plan for the prevention and management of infectious diseases in the municipality. The purpose of establishing this law and the basic plan is to enable the systematic quarantine activities of the national and local governments and to strengthen the linkage between them by suggesting the basic goals and directions for infectious disease prevention and management. A national infectious disease management system developed through this process aims at effective prevention of transmission and risk communication of outbreak of new infectious disease, and the main elements are as follows: (i) declaration and reporting, (ii) monitoring and epidemiological investigation, (iii) vaccination, (iv) blocking the transmission of infection, and (v) prevention.

**Table 1: First and Second Basic Plan for Infectious Disease Control and Prevention**

|  | First Plan | Second Plan |
|---|---|---|
| **Period** | 2013–2017 | 2018–2022 |
| **Vision** | Protecting the public's safety and health by combating infectious diseases | Ensuring a safe society without worrying about infectious diseases |
| **Purpose** | Fighting infectious diseases and suppressing epidemics<br><br>Suppressing the inflow of infectious diseases from overseas<br><br>Minimizing damage by strengthening the ability to respond to new infectious diseases | Reinforcing early detection of infectious diseases and rapid response<br><br>Preventing and managing infectious disease risk factors<br><br>Strengthening infectious disease management organization and system |
| **Main tasks** | Improving initial response ability<br><br>Expanding vaccination support<br><br>Strengthening capacity to prepare for and respond to public health crises<br><br>Improving patient safety and advanced medical-related infection management<br><br>Customizing response and risk communication for each infectious disease<br><br>Promoting international cooperation<br><br>Fostering the bio-industry based on disease management and contributing to the creative economy | Reinforcing infectious disease response and preparation system<br><br>Establishing "one health" cooperation system<br><br>Reinforcing infectious disease prevention and management measures<br><br>Building a technology innovation platform to response for infectious diseases<br><br>Reinforcing infectious disease response and preparation infrastructure |

Source: Ministry of Health and Welfare, KCDC (Korea Centers for Disease Control and Prevention).

In addition, the government, led by the Ministry of Health and Welfare (MOHW), has created and is operating a standard manual (first established on 31 August 2010 by the Korea Centers for Disease Control and Prevention (KCDC); the department in charge was changed to the MOHW from 2014) for risk management that can respond to an outbreak of an infectious disease. This manual was prepared to help prevent harm to the public health due to infectious diseases, and to suggest a pan-government crisis management system and direction of activities for each institution.

The outbreak crisis of new infectious diseases abroad such as COVID-19 is managed through a crisis warning system classified into four stages (attention–caution–alert–serious) according to the scale and speed of transmission (Figure 1). The system provides guidance about which actions are taken by the central and which ones by the local government. Details of the division of responsibility between the central and local government is described below. The main response principles at each level are surveillance (at the attention level), containment (at the caution level), and mitigation (at the alert and serious levels). The basic goals of the crisis management response system caused by new infectious diseases such as the COVID-19 pandemic are to (i) establish preparedness against infectious disease disasters; (ii) effectively respond and block further transmission; and (iii) disclose prompt, accurate, and transparent information to reduce public anxiety.

## Figure 1: Four Stages of Crisis Warning System Under the Situation of New Infectious Disease

| Stage | Situation | Response System | |
|---|---|---|---|
| | | Central Government | Local Government |
| Attention | Outbreak and epidemic of new infectious diseases abroad | KCDC Countermeasures Group | in the affected region Quarantine Countermeasure Group |
| Caution | Domestic influx of new infectious diseases abroad | KCDC Central Disease Control Headquarters | in all regions Quarantine Countermeasure Group |
| Alert | Limited spread of new infectious diseases in the Republic of Korea | KCDC Central Disease Control Headquarters — MOHW Central Disaster Management Headquarters — MOSPA Pan-governmental Response Center | in the affected region Local Disaster and Safety Counter measure Headquarters — in all regions Quarantine Countermeasure Group |
| Serious | Local community dissemination or nationwide spread of new infectious diseases in the Republic of Korea | KCDC Central Disease Control Headquarters — Central Disaster and Safety Countermeasure Headquarters MOHW Central Disaster Management Headquarters MOSPA Pan-governmental Response Center | in all regions Local Disaster and Safety Countermeasure Headquarters — in all regions Quarantine Countermeasure Group |

KCDC = Korea Centers for Disease Control and Prevention, MOHW = Ministry of Health and Welfare, MOSPA = Ministry of Public Administration and Security.

Source: Author.

# 2.2 Structure

**KEY MESSAGE**

*Based on experience, the Government of the Republic of Korea established a support system for infectious disease management through public–private partnerships to strengthen regional response capabilities in the event of an infectious disease outbreak. The Korea Centers for Disease Control and Prevention (KCDC) was promoted as an agency– Korea Disease Control and Prevention Agency (KDCA)–to cope with the crisis more efficiently. The agency has jurisdiction over six laws including the Act on the Prevention of Infectious Diseases, along with the authority to execute them. A 24-hour monitoring facility was established to strengthen the monitoring of the inflow and outbreak of infectious diseases. This helped the crisis response analysts to handle the pandemic with predictions through analyzed information. Further development in infectious disease research and development (R&D) is anticipated through strengthened R&D organizations. For example, the Infectious Diseases Research Center was expanded and reorganized to the National Infectious Diseases Research Institute along with the promotion to KDCA.*

During the H1N1 influenza epidemic, the ROK struggled with the lack of experienced experts in managing infectious diseases. Due to the influence of the Korean medical system in which private medical institutions are in charge of the functions of public medical care, most of the medical treatment and technical support work was performed by private medical institutions at the time. Based on these experiences, the government had tried to establish a support system for infectious disease management through public–private partnerships to strengthen regional response capabilities in the event of an infectious disease outbreak. For this, an efficient and dedicated organization at the national level was needed above all to support the response strategy of KCDC (Figure 2). First, by installing the Infectious Disease Control Center for each region, led by KCDC, a medical delivery system integrating administrative divisions was established (a pilot project in 2011). As a result, the local government's Infectious Disease Control Center, comprising private sector experts to manage infectious diseases and to respond quickly was established. The Infectious Disease Control Center was first established in Seoul in 2012, and as of September 2020, the Infectious Disease Control Center has operated infectious disease management support groups in eight cities across the country. The central government plans to expand support groups to 17 provinces nationwide by 2022.

The main body of infectious disease management comprises the infectious disease management department of each province, and local universities and hospitals are entrusted to carry out capacity-building projects to manage infectious diseases. The center conducts infectious disease outbreak simulation training, establishes a response system, and trains experts to manage infectious disease. The Infectious Disease Control Center provides sentinel surveillance, epidemiologic investigation, education, facility management, and policy advice. However, in the event of a crisis, it is converted into an organization that manages local epidemics. It is currently being used as a window for important private cooperation in the current COVID-19 outbreak, and it conducts epidemiological investigations and data analysis in the region, establishing a response system, and consulting activities. The organization and main tasks of the support group are basically the same, but the composition and size of the support group in each region are slightly different depending on the epidemic pattern of infectious diseases.

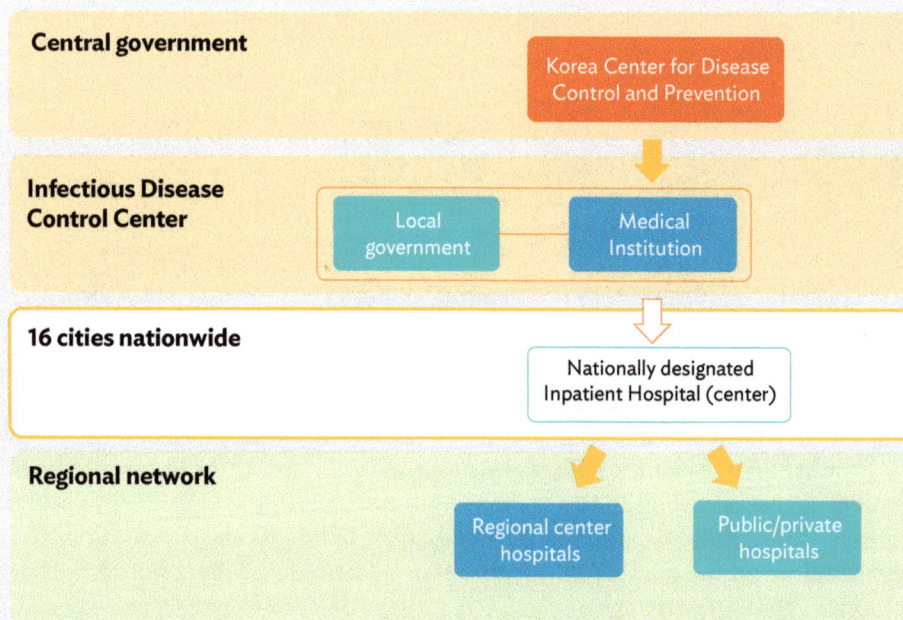

**Figure 2: Structure of Regional Public–Private Network for Infectious Disease Crisis Response**

Source: Adapted from Ajou University. 2013. *Report for 2012 Public Health Crisis Response Project Operation*. 1 February.

In the case of the Seoul center, the Planning Management Team, Crisis Response Team, and Community Capacity Building Team are supported by the leader and vice-captain. The Steering Committee and Standing Advisory Committee are formed on a part-time basis. In addition, the nonexecutive advisory committee provides direction in responding to infectious diseases and information disclosure.

Second, regional center hospitals, which had been fostered for expanding local public health care, were included in the network for infectious disease crisis management. In the event of an infectious disease epidemic, these hospitals closely cooperated with KCDC and regional infectious disease control centers to mitigate low-risk patients.

Quarantine treatment facilities for high-risk patients in infectious disease epidemic areas were temporarily created through larger regional and more specialized medical institutions (2019). If this system is converted to a more permanent operation, it is expected that the containment and management of local high-risk patients will be strengthened.

After the Crisis Alert Level of COVID-19 was raised to Level 4 as of 23 February 2020, the Government of the ROK created the Central Disaster and Safety Countermeasure Headquarters, a response system headed by the Prime Minister for a wider, national-level response (Figure 3). Considering the expertise required for this pandemic, the Central Disease Control Headquarters (KCDC) acts as a central command center to prevent and control infectious diseases. Each of the two vice-heads of the Central Disaster and Safety Countermeasure Headquarters assists the Central Disease Control Headquarters. The first deputy head serves as the head of the Central Disaster Management Headquarters (minister of health and welfare) focusing on preventive measures and quarantine work, whereas the head of Pan-Government Countermeasures Support Headquarters (minister of interior and safety) takes the role of second deputy head, helping coordination between the central and local governments. The Local Disaster and Safety Management Headquarters is then established by each local government. The heads of the local government collaborate to ensure an adequate number of beds, personnel, and supplies, joining forces with each local infectious disease prevention and control team.

## Figure 3: The Republic of Korea Response System

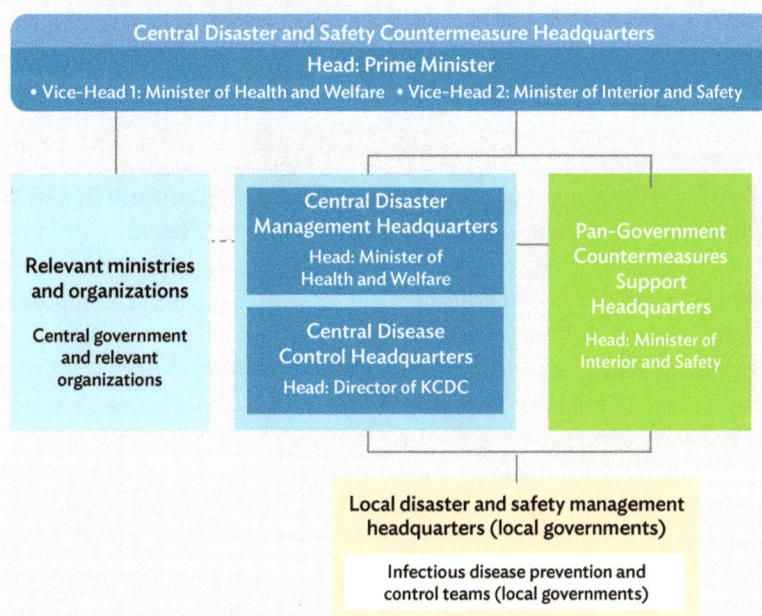

KCDC = Korea Centers for Disease Control and Prevention.
Source: Ministry of Health and Welfare of the Republic of Korea, 2020.

## Promotion of Korea Centers for Disease Control and Prevention to Korea Disease Control and Prevention Agency

Because of the second wave of COVID-19, which had a high possibility of occurring during the second half of 2020, the government prioritized the promotion and capacity enhancement of KCDC. ROK President Moon Jae-in announced the promotion of the KCDC to KDCA in a special speech marking his third anniversary of inauguration. This aimed to lay the foundation for empowerment the public health-care system and the ability to respond to infectious diseases. General objectives included strengthening professionalism and independence of KCDC, expanding the number of professionals in the center, and introducing a multiple vice-minister system to the MOHW (Office of the President 2020).

The 45th State Council on 8 September 2020 voted on the Revision of the MOHW, the Partial Revision of the Organization of Health and Welfare and its Affiliates, and the Proposal for the Directions for the Period of the Disease Control and Prevention. KCDC was officially promoted from a center to an agency on 12 September. As a member of the MOHW, KCDC did not have independent authority over the organization, personnel, and budget, which limited the available expertise and prevented the establishment of an infectious disease policy department. During the COVID-19 pandemic, several quarters pointed out that it was difficult for KCDC to play the role of a command tower as responsible departments are scattered among the MOHW, the Office of the President, and the Ministry of Public Safety and Security. Now reorganized as an agency, KDCA has jurisdiction over six laws including the Act on the Prevention of Infectious Diseases along with the authority to execute them (KDCA 2020).

Main changes took effect due to the promotion. The number of new staff is 384, which is 42% of the existing quota excluding the personnel relocated to the transfer between the KCDC and the Health and Welfare district. This expansion on the number of faculties aims to enhance practical functions of KDCA. A 24-hour monitoring facility was established to strengthen the monitoring of the inflow and outbreak of infectious diseases 24 hours a day; this assists the crisis response analysts to handle the pandemic with predictions through analyzed information. A further development in infectious disease R&D is anticipated through strengthened R&D organizations along with the promotion to KDCA. The Infectious Diseases Research Center, which belonged to the National Institute of Health under the KCDC, was expanded and reorganized to establish the National Infectious Diseases Research Institute. The research center will have its own R&D system for infectious diseases including vaccine development support, as well as research on infectious viruses (Ministry of the Interior and Safety 2020b).

Another significant change is the installment of the Centers for Disease Response in five areas (metropolitan Seoul, Chungcheong, Honam, Gyeongbuk, and Gyeongnam) to cope with diseases in a more localized context considering region-specific risks. Establishing policies are important, but to respond well on-site is another significant factor in dealing with the risk. The centers conduct surveys to monitor and prepare vulnerable areas in the region, and assist local governments to support epidemiological investigations, diagnosis, and analysis, which is difficult for local governments to handle due to lack of capacity. Human resources will also be added to allow cooperation between the center and the local government. Operating a consultative body on a regular basis for sharing policy information is another goal to increase the efficiency in coping with the crisis.

In addition, under the revision of the Government Organization Act in August 2020, the MOHW will appoint a second vice-minister in charge of health and medical services. The previous vice-minister will handle welfare, while the second vice-minister will be responsible for health and medical care. The promotion of KCDC to KDCA means that an independent administrative agency, which has greatly enhanced expertise has been established (Office of the President 2020). This reorganization will be enforced 1 month after the promulgation of the legislative bill. Given the practical authority, the agency can establish a close and organic response network for infectious disease response and prevention. Furthermore, the transition in local infectious disease response system will allow the local governments to cooperate in response to the crisis, reinforcing their protection of local communities. The second vice-minister in the Ministry of Health can actively communicate with the medical community and National Assembly by gathering opinions for preparing health protection solutions, narrowing the medical gap between regions. During the health crisis, the reorganization of KCDC serves as an opportunity to strengthen the nation's public health and medical capabilities (Office of the President, 2020).

## 2.3 Legal System

**KEY MESSAGE**

*The Infectious Disease Control and Prevention Act was enacted in the Republic of Korea in 2010 for more effective responsive measures to infectious diseases based on earlier experiences. The constant revision of relevant statutes, which followed changes and reflected on-site feedback, implies that building a legal framework for standardized responses to a crisis is critical in turning that crisis into a more manageable situation.*

With lessons learned from SARS of 2003 and MERS of 2015, the legislative system has also played a significant role in the response to COVID-19 in the ROK (Figure 4). While confirmed cases of SARS in the country did not reach a high number, it affected the overall national framework for infectious disease control, leading to the launch of KCDC to a new standardized control body. MERS cost more difficulties as the control system did not function efficiently and effectively in both prevention and response, recording 186 confirmed cases and 38 deaths in total. Opaque information on confirmed cases and the sluggish response of the central government not only aroused distrust and anxiety of the public, but also actually increased the number of infected people. From this financial perspective, the revised Infectious Disease Control and Prevention Act of Republic of Korea in 2015 mainly dealt with assuring transparency and rapidness of information transfer and more efficient allocation of material and human resources. The revision was acknowledged for (i) establishing prompt and effective response system to infectious diseases, (ii) releasing information on outbreaks of infectious diseases, and (iii) clarifying obligation of patients and rationales for its compensation (MOHW 2015).

This statute has been at the center of COVID-19 responses as well. Transparent disclosure of information and centralized control management, in particular, led to successful responses at the initial stage. The provision itself and other legislations, however, went through major changes after the outbreak of COVID-19. The first step was the amendment of three bills for rapid responses of COVID-19, which were passed at the Parliament on 26 February. They were urgently deliberated on to strengthen a national-level capacity for infectious disease control and relieve public anxiety on COVID-19. The main contents and expected effects of each law are as follows (MOHW 2020a): (i) revision of the Infectious Disease Control and Prevention Act was for responsive measures to suspected patients, regulation on the flow of medical supplies to abroad, and strengthening overall capacity of epidemiological investigation; and (ii) the Quarantine Act was revised so that legal basis can be clarified for requests on prohibition of entry or departure to anyone who is infected or suspected to be infected with infectious disease. Nationals of the ROK were excluded from this. Finally, by amending the Medical Service Act, more effective monitoring on infection within health-care or medical facilities was expected.

## Box 2: Disease Control and Prevention Act of Republic of Korea in 2015

Following the global epidemic of the severe acute respiratory syndrome (SARS) in 2003, the World Health Organization (WHO) hastened to amend the International Health Regulations (IHR) and adopted IHR 2005 formally at a plenary meeting in May 2005. In IHR 2005, WHO broadened the scope of disease quarantine to "a disease or medical condition that can cause significant damage to a person regardless of cause or source," and recommended each member state to have core competencies for disease surveillance and response within 5 years. In response to this, the relevant laws were reorganized in the Republic of Korea, and the government announced the Infectious Disease Control and Prevention Act in December 2009 and implemented it in December 2010. In addition, two revisions were made to improve the problem of the new infectious disease quarantine system revealed through the 2015 Middle East respiratory syndrome (MERS) outbreak. The main contents of the Infectious Disease Control and Prevention Act (2015) are as follows.

- Designation notifiable diseases: Adding new overseas infectious diseases.
- Duties and rights: Duties of state and local governments (the dignity and values of patients); medical personnel (cooperate with the state and local governments that perform the affairs of the surveillance, prevention, and control of the outbreak of infectious diseases and epidemiological investigations); and citizens (cooperate with the State and local governments) and citizens' rights (the right to know information on the situation of the outbreak of infectious diseases and the prevention and control of infectious diseases).
- Master plan and projects: Formulation of prevention and control plans of infectious diseases (nurturing professional manpower, strengthening crisis response capabilities by type of medical institution, sharing information between medical institutions); operation of organizations supporting infectious disease control projects and the infectious disease control committee; etc.
- Notification and reporting: Defines a person liable for a report and report target (heads of Public Health Clinics).
- Surveillance and epidemiologic investigation: Sentinel surveillance, fact-finding surveys, epidemiological investigations, medical examinations, autopsy orders, etc.
- Prevent spread: Formulation and implementation of crisis control measures (conduct regular training and information disclosure), designation and establishment of infectious disease control institutions, establishing and managing infectious disease control facilities, duty of business owners to cooperate with quarantine, compulsory dispositions, etc.
- Preventive measures: The minister of education or the superintendent of education orders the school to close, or in consultation with the minister of health and welfare to order the closure of educational facilities.
- Provision of materials and information: Request for information on (i) installation and operation of management facilities/containment facilities/clinics to the head of an infectious disease management institution, (ii) persons concerned with infection to the police agency, and (iii) persons concerned about infection by the police agency to the information service provider and telecommunication service provider; the collected information is used only to prevent spread of infection, destroy the information after the end of the business (notify the minister of Health and Welfare), penalties for disapproving the request for information provision, etc.
- Expenses and compensation for losses: Expenses to be borne by special self-governing provinces and Sis/Guns/ Gus, Cites/Dos, and National Treasury.

Sources: B.C. Chun. 2011. Public Policy and Laws on Infectious Disease Control in Korea; Past, Present and Prospective. *Infect Chemother*. 43 (6): 474–484; D.H. Lee and K. Park. 2005. Revision of international health regulation and task of improving communicable disease control and quarantine system in the Republic of Korea. *J Korean Med Association*. 48: 784–94; World Health Organization. 2008. *International Health Regulations (2005)*. 2nd edition.

## Figure 4: Timeline of the Legislative Changes for the Management of New Infectious Diseases

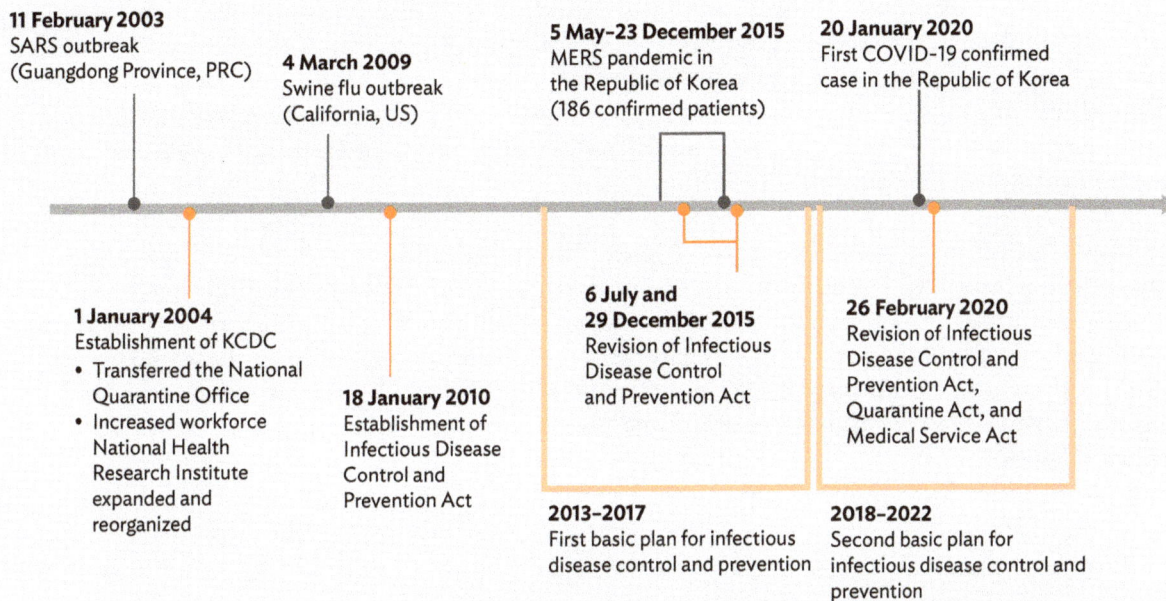

**11 February 2003**
SARS outbreak
(Guangdong Province, PRC)

**4 March 2009**
Swine flu outbreak
(California, US)

**5 May–23 December 2015**
MERS pandemic in
the Republic of Korea
(186 confirmed patients)

**20 January 2020**
First COVID-19 confirmed
case in the Republic of Korea

**1 January 2004**
Establishment of KCDC
- Transferred the National
  Quarantine Office
- Increased workforce
  National Health
  Research Institute
  expanded and
  reorganized

**18 January 2010**
Establishment of
Infectious Disease
Control and
Prevention Act

**6 July and
29 December 2015**
Revision of Infectious
Disease Control
and Prevention Act

**2013–2017**
First basic plan for infectious
disease control and prevention

**26 February 2020**
Revision of Infectious
Disease Control and
Prevention Act,
Quarantine Act, and
Medical Service Act

**2018–2022**
Second basic plan for
infectious disease control and
prevention

COVID-19 = coronavirus disease, KCDC = Korea Centers for Disease Control and Prevention, MERS = Middle East respiratory syndrome, SARS = severe acute respiratory syndrome, US = United States.
Source: Author.

The second legislative step took place on 4 August, passing the Infectious Disease Control and Prevention Act (MOHW 2020b). This mainly targeted required measures that should be taken immediately on-site. The projected results included (i) ordering compliance with the preventive measures against infectious disease and enabling imposition of fines, (ii) defraying treatment expenses for those infected abroad, and (iii) differentiating the level of treatment on the basis of severity of the disease.

The most recent change was also made within Infectious Disease Control and Prevention Act, which was to supplement necessary measures that were required on-site (MOHW, 2020c). The goal was to respond intensely and effectively to prolonged situations under the pandemic, particularly considering the country's national holidays (Chuseok), increased traveling that can ensue, and possible growth of risk during the winter season. By this revision, (i) the head of local government is granted authority to order the suspension of operation of a facility or area that has potential to transmit infectious diseases and did not comply with preventive measures, (ii) grounds are established for surveillance of the highest level suspected infected people who are in quarantine, and (iii) more intensified preventive measures on patients and medical staffs are arranged from a long-term perspective.

The constant revision of relevant statues, which took into account events and reflected on-site feedback, implies that building a legal framework for standardized responses to a crisis is critical in turning that crisis into a more manageable situation.

To go into further details on the legal basis, the latest version of Coronavirus Disease 2019 Response Guidelines (for local governments) distributed by the Central Disease Control Headquarters and the Central Disaster Management Headquarters, mainly focuses on Infectious Disease Control and Prevention Act. Articles on

"Epidemiological investigation" and "Management of patients and close contacts" were significant in this sense. Article 18 on "Epidemiological investigation" does not permit anyone to "(a) refuse, interfere with, evade the epidemiological investigation without justifiable ground (b) make a false statement or present false materials (c) intentionally omit or conceal any facts" and Article 79 states that "[v]iolation may result in up to 2 years in prison or a fine of up to 20 million won." Article 35-2 on "Management of patients and close contacts" makes it clear that "no one is permitted to make a false statement, intentionally omit or conceal any facts, etc. to medical personnel regarding visits to healthcare facilities and diagnoses/treatments, etc." Article 83 states that "[v]iolation may result in a fine of up to 10 million won" (The Central Disease Control Headquarters & The Central Disaster Management Headquarters, 2020).

The Infectious Disease Control and Prevention Act also provides legal ground for efficient and effective management of the disease by articles on "On-site management," "Preventive measures," "On-site command," "Provision of information," "Funerary methods," "Employers' obligation to cooperate," "Compulsory measures regarding infectious disease," and "Temporary duty orders." It further handles support for those who are under hardship due to the disease by dealing with "Compensation for losses," "Financial support for medical professionals and owners of healthcare facilities," and "Livelihood assistance for patients and others with infectious disease."

# 2.4  Local Governance

## KEY MESSAGE

*One of the goals of forming local governance as a component of the Central Disaster and Safety Countermeasure Headquarters is to promote coordination in work among central and local governments. Therefore, infectious disease prevention and control teams are established in cities and districts where outbreaks occur. The local government provides administrative support from test result management to the supervision of environment, facilities, and resources.*

The operation of the KCDC as well as the Central Disaster Management Headquarters as an affiliated organization of the MOHW, Local Disaster and Safety Management Headquarters is under the authority of local governments. Infectious disease prevention and control teams are established in the cities and districts where outbreaks occur.

One of the goals of forming local governance as a component of the Central Disaster and Safety Countermeasure Headquarters is to promote coordination between the central and local governments. As a way of enhancing cooperation, the central–local working level consultation body is organized under the deputy head of Central Disaster Management Headquarters (Government of the ROK 2020).

The local governance responding to the disease entails the formation and operation of a city or province immediate response team within the regional quarantine task force (Central Disease Control Headquarters Central Disaster Management Headquarters 2020). Centered on the city where infectious cases had occurred, the immediate response team investigates epidemiological cases of confirmed patients, their contacts, and the management of environmental measures. In cases where additional patients or multiple contacts have appeared in a collective facility, the team advices on how to operate the system. The city or province immediate response team consists of about five to seven people who act as disaster officers and perform epidemiological surveys, on-site control and management of contact data, administration, and inspection. The operation is flexible depending on the analyzed situation of the local government, which leads to timely investigation and response.

The system allows information on cases of the infectious disease to be relayed to the city, province, and KCDC for integrated management. In 2007, KCDC reorganized the reporting system of infectious disease and the legal infectious disease statistics information system based on the web. Once aware of cases of the disease, hospitals or health centers immediately phone the city, province, and the KCDC and report the occurrence into the integrated disease and health management system. The same applies for confirmed patients (including death). Positive test results should be reported on the same day. The emergency operating center in KCDC provides the confirmed number of patients for the reported cases of the day.

The city or province immediate response team plays a vital role after the confirmation of the cases (Figure 5). The task force of where the case has first been recognized takes charge of its epidemiological investigation. In contact investigation and management, the health center that confirmed the case conducts a contact survey under the direction of corresponding immediate response team. The team of the actual residential area of the patient later takes over the management of the case after the contact list is registered in the system. Furthermore, risk assessment of collective facilities or medical institutions in each region is also one of the main duties for the city and provincial immediate response team, including the decisions on whether the facility should be closed if the risk of infection is significantly high. The management plan is established based on the evaluation of the exposure situation, facilities, environment, and operation personnel collected from field investigation results (Central

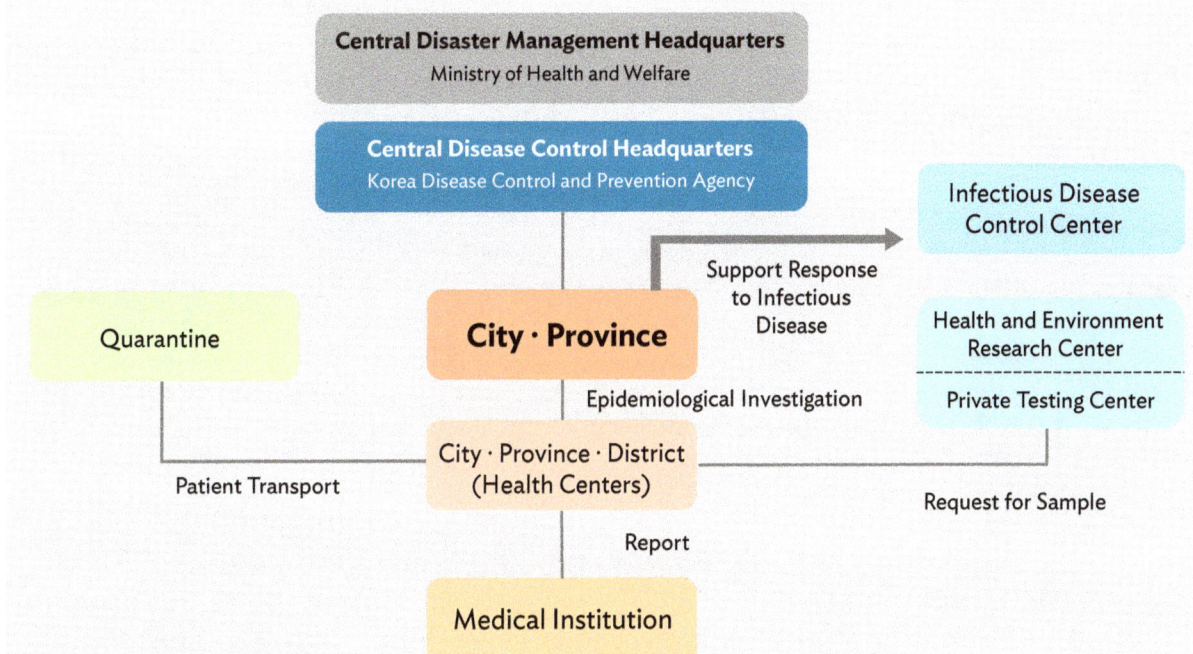

**Figure 5: Roles of Central and Local Institutions**

Source: Central Disaster Control Headquarters, Central Disaster Management Headquarters, 2020.

Disease Control Headquarters & Central Disaster Management Headquarters 2020). Local Disaster and Safety Management Headquarters forms and supports a field-specific support team (differing by quarantine, medical support, living support, and on-site control) based on the on-site assessment as well.

Local government participates in providing administrative support from test result management to the supervision of environment, facilities, and resources. In the case of resource management, the guidelines are applied flexibly depending on the situation of each region, which is why cooperation among local governments is significant. For patient care, the city and province have established teams to identify the accurate number of available sickbeds, hospitals, and medical resources. The availability of "negative pressure rooms" is also another factor to investigate when scrutinizing the intensive care units for patients. There is a procedure for patient flow between cities and provinces, which allows the local governments to facilitate communication while handling the outbreak of the infectious diseases.

# 2.5  Public–Private Partnership

**KEY MESSAGE**

*Public–private partnership (PPP) has been pivotal in both the prevention and response system of the Republic of Korea, from tracking infection cases to eventual development of testing kits and further research and development (R&D) work. The government's R&D investment over the last years and the emergency use authorization system made rapid development of test kits possible. When it comes to treatment, a PPP was formed to support R&D and clinical trials. Partnership between the public and private sectors has developed into more organizational cooperation as well, with the prolonged situation.*

Public–private partnership (PPPs) and collaboration have also been critical in building responsive framework of the ROK. For swift treatment and prevention of possible infection, hospitals and pharmacies could have access to patients' travel histories. Government-designated institutions, regional hub hospitals, and national infectious disease hospitals were allocated to confirmed patients for more efficient treatment. Private hospitals have set their priority on providing care to COVID-19 cases as well, cooperating with governmental bodies.

Clinical testing and R&D of vaccines and therapies were pushed in collaboration with the private sector. Research on diagnostic agents, therapies, clinical epidemiology, and vaccines were conducted through the distribution of research resources from February 2020, with notification of research tasks, conduct of emergency response research, and cooperation with the private sector. The government R&D investment over the last years and the emergency use authorization system made rapid development of test kits possible. As of 2017, the government had invested W28.6 billion in R&D of the infectious disease diagnosis technology (Ministry of Science and ICT [MSICT]: W15.9 billion; Ministry of Trade, Industry and Energy: W3.2 billion; MHOW: W6.5 billion) (MSICT 2020) (Table 2).

When it comes to treatment, a PPP was formed to support R&D and clinical trials. A drug repositioning council and a pan-government support group for the development of a treatment and vaccine against COVID-19 were launched in February and April, respectively. An R&D consultation body consisting of government-funded research institutes and the four major institutes of science and technology (Korea Advanced Institute of Science and Technology, Daegu Gyeongbuk Institute of Science and Technology, Ulsan National Institute of Science and Technology, and Gwangju Institute of Science and Technology) was formed to provide various services to treatment and vaccine development companies (MSICT 2020).

**Table 2: Ministry of Science and Information Technology Support for Companies That Obtained Emergency Use Approvals**

| Company | Category | Project and Government Funding |
|---|---|---|
| KogeneBiotech | Molecular diagnostics | Development of diagnostic technology for mosquito-borne viruses using Multiplex PCR (2015–2020); a total of W23.1 billion provided |
| SolGent | Molecular diagnostics | Development of detection kits for Zika/Dengue/Chikurgunya viruses (2016–2019); a total of W20.5 billion provided |
| SD Biosensor | Molecular diagnostics | Development of diagnosis technology for Zika/Dengue/Chikurgunya viruses based on PCR for isothermal nucleic acid amplification (2016–2019); a total of W8.5 billion provided |

PCR = Polymerase Chain Reaction.

Source: How We Fought COVID-19: A Perspective from Science & ICT, Ministry of Science and ICT, 2020.

The government eased the burden on micro, small, and medium-sized enterprises (MSMEs) participating in government R&D projects and provided support for their labor costs. The government plans to cut royalties for companies and made R&D regulations more flexible. Burden reductions on private sector by ministry (cash payments) are: Ministry of Science and Technology Information and Communication (MSIT): W42.6 billion (cash payment, W13.7 billion); Ministry of Trade Industry and Energy: W653.8 billion (cash payment, W511.7 billion); and Ministry of SMEs and Startups : W296 billion (cash payment, W296 billion) (MSICT 2020) (Figure 6).

Rapid approval of a diagnostic testing kit was one of the successful outcomes of PPP. The partnership was established even before the first confirmed case within the country, as they sought rapid development of testing kit using real-time polymerase chain reaction (RT-PCR) technology. The developed kits then went through expedited approval to be used for suspected cases, by the Food and Drug Administration of the ROK by mid-January. Diagnostic tools including these testing kits production had to scale up as the situation worsened. Actual deployment was practiced rapidly, thanks to the partnerships with local government bodies.

**Figure 6: Changes to Ratio of Burden on Research Costs and Cash Payment of Medium-Sized Enterprises**

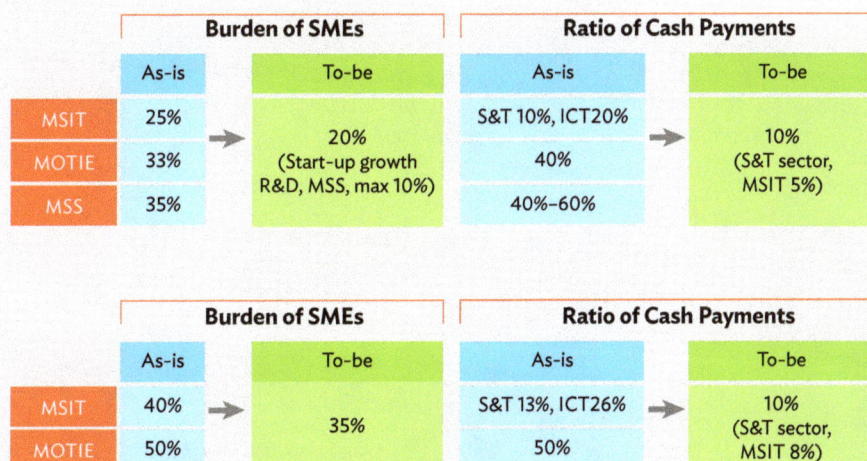

ICT = information and communication technology, MOTIE = Ministry of Trade Industry and Energy, MSIT = Ministry of Science and ICT, MSS = Ministry of SMEs and Startups, SMEs = small and medium-sized enterprises, S&T = science and technology.

Source: How We Fought COVID-19: A Perspective from Science & ICT, Ministry of Science and ICT, 2020. p. 94.

This aggressive testing and tracing capacity, to a large extent, "relied on the rapid engagement of the private sector and approval of tests by the Korean Food and Drug Administration," which eventually "facilitated earlier and more effective containment of viral spread compared with other countries" (Oh et al. 2020). Testing had proven to be essential as a component of the 3T—Testing, Tracing, Treatment—which later became core strategies of response system. The central government and health authority cooperated with the private sector as they have known that nationwide installation of Emergency Use Authorization (EUA) process for RT-PCR test sites would require more resources than those of KCDC alone (Park and Chung 2020).  The cost of testing was covered by public health insurance.

By late January 2020, the approval by KCDC led pharmaceutical companies to increase their productions and shipping of COVID-19-related supplies, especially testing kits. As of August, the ROK is one of the largest manufacturers of testing kits. It is estimated that global demand for the kits is about 700,000 a day from more than 110 countries. Scale-up of production and shipping of testing kits were made possible thanks not only to the companies' rapid development of capacity, but also to the government's prompt authorization regarding required procedures (DHL 2020).

Partnership between the public and private sectors has developed into more organizational cooperation as well, with the prolonged situation. Seoul Metropolitan City, for instance, organized a consultative body with 15 hospitals to discuss securing sickbeds while the confirmed cases in the region were surging in August, underscoring the importance of PPP in the medical sector to flatten the curves of the "second wave" (Im 2020). The city also sought the establishment of community treatment centers at private facilities so that it can secure enough facility to accommodate patients or suspected infectees (Seoul Metropolitan Government 2020). It was not only the Seoul Metropolitan City that looked for smooth allocation and securing resources for treatment via partnering outside of the public sector. This is just one of the examples that show significance of PPP in the COVID-19 responses of the country.

PPP has been pivotal in both prevention and response system of the ROK, from tracking infection cases to eventual development of testing kit and further R&D work. While the general success of the ROK during the initial responses to COVID-19 was considered to be the centralized management of national authority, the effectiveness also came from active collaboration of the public and private sectors as well, offering more complementary strategies to the overall framework.

# 3 3T: The Republic of Korea's COVID-19 Response

## 3.1 Testing

**KEY MESSAGE**

*The Republic of Korea (ROK) is equipped with the diagnostic testing capability, thus anyone can take the diagnostic test at any time. Also, establishing the guidelines and terminology helped to feed into the integrated health information management system. Through the Drug Utilization Review/International Traveler Information System, inappropriate drug use can be checked in advance by providing information related to drug safety in real-time to doctors and pharmacists. The screening test for COVID-19 is supported by the government in accordance with Articles 4 and 67 of the Infectious Disease Control and Prevention Act. Open application open interface (API) data provides information on COVID-19 National Safe Hospitals and Screening Centers through a public data portal. Lastly, test kit development through research and development has been very actively implemented in the ROK.*

### Screening Centers

To detect COVID-19 patients early and prevent the transmission of infection in advance, the government and medical institutions have established and are operating screening centers. The screening center is a space where patients with suspected infectious diseases such as cough or fever receive separate treatment before entering a medical institution.

Through this, the accessibility of diagnostic tests for patients has been improved, large-scale rapid diagnostic tests have been made possible, and operating models such as the drive-through and walk-through have also been diversified and operated (Figure 7). It takes about 10 minutes for a patient visiting the drive-through center to complete registration, testing, collection, and instruction. More than 100 tests can be performed per day in one drive-through center and infection between subjects in the waiting area is avoided. A total of 638 health centers and medical institutions have established and are operating screening clinics, of which 95% of them, or 596, directly collect samples (as of 27 September 2020). With these diagnostic testing capabilities, anyone can take the diagnostic test at any time, even if there are no symptoms of infection and no history of contact with an infected person.

## Figure 7: Types of Screening Centers for COVID-19

**Drive-through screening center**

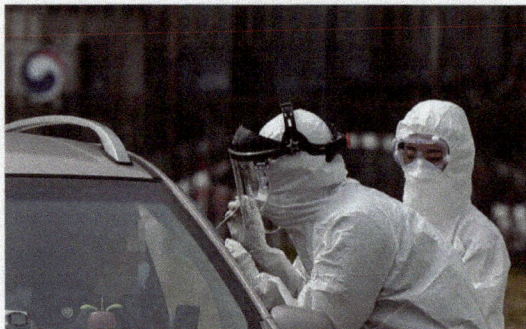

**Walk-through screening center**

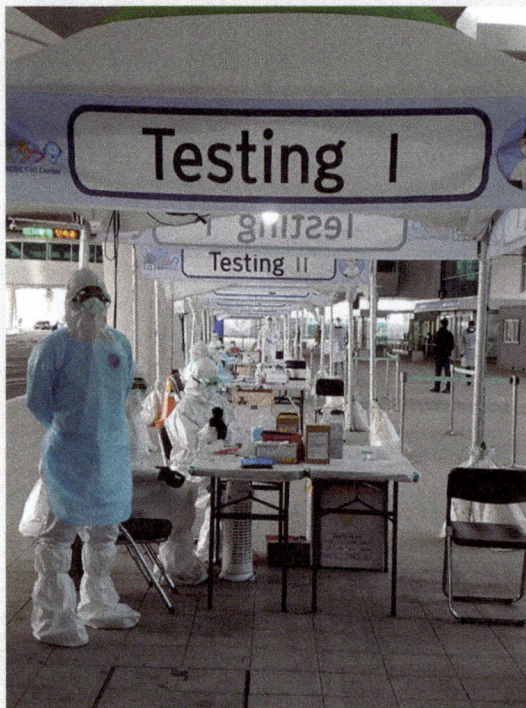

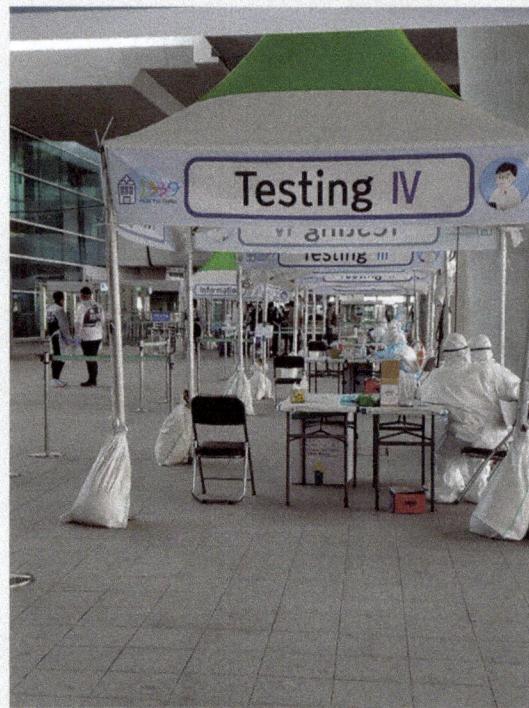

Source: Ministry of Health and Welfare. http://ncov.mohw.go.kr/baroView2.do?brdId=4&brdGubun=42.

### Guidelines

Since the first confirmed cases of COVID-19, quarantine authorities have conducted diagnostic tests on suspected cases.[1] In the guidelines released on 20 February 2020, "Patient Under Investigation" (PUI) was added to the case definition along with case changes for suspected cases. After three additional changes, COVID-19 infected patients and subjects to be tested were classified into Confirmed Case, Suspected Case, and PUI based on test results, clinical symptoms, and contact history (Table 3). Quickly establishing the guidelines and terminology helped to feed into the integrated health information management system.

---

[1]    Including (i) fever or respiratory symptoms within 14 days after visit to the People's Republic of China, (ii) fever or respiratory symptoms within 14 days after close contact with the confirmed patient, or (iii) suspected of having an epidemiological association with COVID-19.

### Table 3: Case Definition for Patient Visiting Screening Centers

| Case Definitions | Until 20 February 2020 | Revised on 20 February 2020 | Revised on 2 March 2020 | Revised on 2 April 2020 |
|---|---|---|---|---|
| **Confirmed case** | A person who has been confirmed to be infected with the infectious disease pathogen according to the diagnostic testing standard, regardless of clinical manifestations | | | |
| **Suspected case** | A person displaying clinical symptoms (fever or respiratory symptoms) within 14 days visiting the People's Republic of China (PRC) <br><br> A person displaying clinical symptoms (fever or respiratory symptoms) within 14 days of contact with a confirmed COVID-19 patient <br><br> Anyone suspected of having an epidemiological association with COVID-19 | A person displaying clinical symptoms (fever or respiratory symptoms) within 14 days visiting the PRC <br><br> A person displaying clinical symptoms (fever or respiratory symptoms) within 14 days of contact with a confirmed COVID-19 patient <br><br> Patients with pneumonia of unknown cause requiring hospitalization according to the opinion of a doctor | A person displaying clinical symptoms within 14 days of contact with a confirmed COVID-19 patient | |
| **Patients Under Investigation (PUI)** | | A person suspected of COVID-19 according to a physician's opinion <br> A person displaying clinical symptoms (fever or respiratory symptoms) within 14 days visiting country or region where COVID-19 occurred. | A person suspected of COVID-19 such as pneumonia of unknown cause according to a physician's opinion <br><br> A person displaying clinical symptoms within 14 days visiting country with regional spread of COVID-19, such as the PRC; Hong Kong, China; and Macau, China. <br><br> A person exhibiting clinical symptoms of COVID-19 within 14 days with an epidemiological link to a domestic COVID-19 cluster | A person suspected of COVID-19 such as pneumonia of unknown cause according to a physician's opinion <br><br> A person with an overseas travel history displaying clinical symptoms of COVID-19 within 14 days upon entry to the Republic of Korea <br><br> A person exhibiting clinical symptoms of COVID-19 within 14 days with an epidemiological link to a domestic COVID-19 cluster |

COVID-19 = coronavirus disease.

Sources: Central Disease Control Headquarters, COVID-19 Response Guidelines (for local governments), the 6th edition (2 Feb 2020); Central Disease Control Headquarters, COVID-19 Response Guidelines (for local governments), the 7th edition (2 March 2020); Central Disease Control Headquarters, COVID-19 Response Guidelines (for local governments), the 7th-4th edition (2 April 2020).

The major clinical symptoms that are medically suspected of infection with COVID-19 as the standard for conducting diagnostic tests include fever (above 37.5°C), cough, shortness of breath, chills, muscle pain, headache, sore throat, loss of smell and taste, or pneumonia.

Patients who visit the screening centers are classified into Suspected Case and PUI according to clinical symptoms and visit history at the reception stage (Figure 8), and the response procedure after case classification is as follows:

(i)    Response procedure in suspected case
   (a)    Patient transfer - Move the patient to an isolation space or an independent space (if there is no isolation space)
   (b)    Test - Conduct a diagnostic test (COVID-19 [PCR] test)
   (c)    Report - Report the occurrence of a suspected case to the health authorities
   (d)    Patient isolation - Isolation of facilities or hospitals (based on risk and severity)

(ii)    Response procedure in PUI
   (a)    Patient transfer - Move the patient to an isolation space or an independent space (if there is no isolation space)
   (b)    Test - Conduct a diagnostic test (COVID-19 (PCR) test)
   (c)    Report - Report the occurrence of a PUI to the health authorities

### Figure 8: Protocol for Patients Visiting the COVID-19 Screening Centers

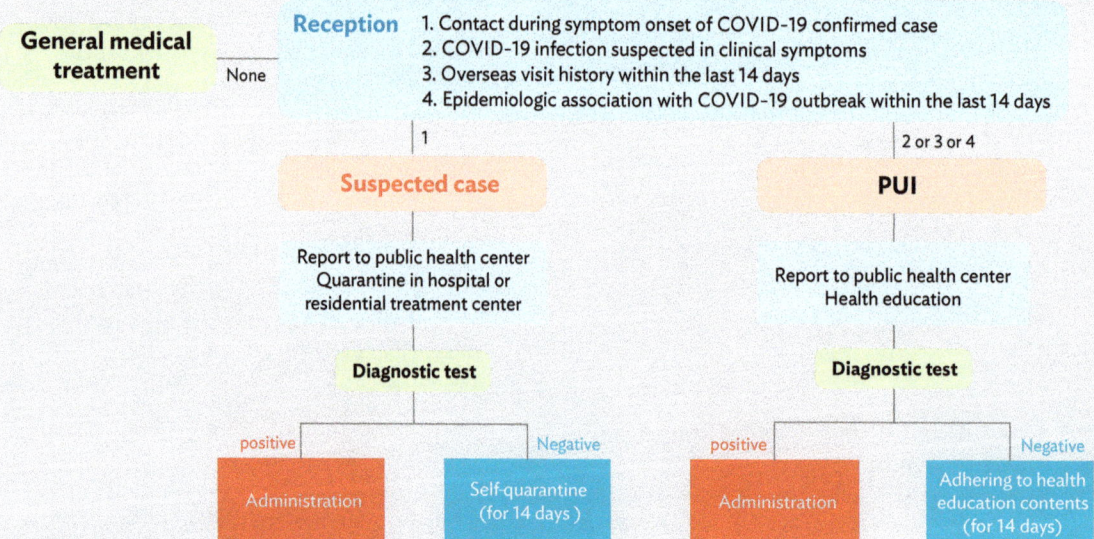

COVID-19 = coronavirus disease, PUI = patient under investigation.
Source: Modified from the webpage operated by the Ministry of Health and Welfare (http://ncov.mohw.go.kr/).

## Implementation

(a)  Drug Utilization Review/International Traveler Information System

Drug Utilization Review (DUR) is a system supported by the Health Insurance Review and Assessment Service (HIRA) so that inappropriate drug use can be checked in advance by providing information related to drug safety in real-time to doctors and pharmacists. When the doctor transmits the patient's prescription information to the system in the prescribing stage, the patient's previous medication history and DUR criteria are compared and checked in real-time. If an abnormal drug is prescribed, a warning message appears on the doctor's monitor screen within 0.5 seconds. The same process goes through when a pharmacist prepares medicine. In the DUR, there is an Overseas Travel History Information Program (the International Traveler Information System [ITS]) that can check visit history for a contaminated area. If an immigrant from an infectious disease outbreak area visits a medical institution, the system provides information on overseas travel for 14 days from the date of entry. At the screening centers, information on entering the country from abroad (provision period: 21 days), contact history of confirmed patients (provision period: 21 days), and release from quarantine after confirmation (provision period: 14 days) are received through DUR/ITS system at the reception stage (Figure 9). Since such information can be provided, the efficiency and accuracy of the first visit can be improved.

**Figure 9: Flowchart for Providing Information on Overseas Travel History Using Drug Utilization Review and/or International Traveler Information System**

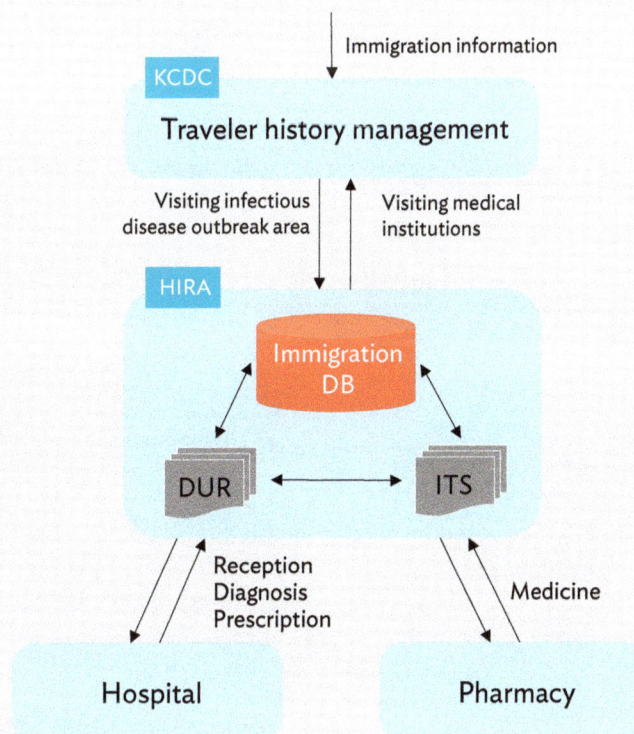

DUR= Drug Utilization Review, HIRA = Health Insurance Review and Assessment Service, ITS = International Traveler Information System, KCDC = Korea Centers for Disease Control and Prevention

Source: Modified from Health insurance review & assessment policy brief 2020; 14(2)) p. 25. http://www.hira.or.kr/co/search.do ?categoryFlag=n&checkSearchFields=ALL&collection=cms_new&cookieonoff=on&period=ETC&query=%ED%98%B8%ED%9 D%A1%EA%B8%B0%ED%95%99%ED%9A%8C&realQuery=%ED%98%B8%ED%9D%A1%EA%B8%B0%ED%95%99%ED%9A %8C&sort=DESC&startCount=0&tapMoveCheck=1

**Box 3: Drug Utilization Review System**

The Drug Utilization Review (DUR) is the only system in the world that checks the patient's medication history in real-time, and provides uninterrupted service 24 hours a day, 365 days a year. The system supports the people's safe use of medicines, and at the same time, enables the operation of a national drug surveillance network by grasping the real-time usage history of drugs in an epidemic outbreak. In particular, the International Traveler Information System, which the Korean Center for Disease Control developed and started to use for rapid initial response to infectious diseases during the Middle East Respiratory Syndrome outbreak in 2015, can help early diagnosis of infectious diseases because it is linked with an electronic medical record to provide information, at the reception stage, on patients visiting contaminated areas.

Source: Webpage for DUR operated by Health Insurance Review and Assessment Service. https://www.hira.or.kr/dummy. do?pgmid=HIRAA990001000330.

(b)    National Support of Screening Cost

The screening test for COVID-19 is supported by the government in accordance with Articles 4 and 67 of the Infectious Disease Control and Prevention Act. Support targets include patients with suspicious symptoms of COVID-19 infection, those who have entered the country from abroad, those who have come into contact with confirmed cases, and those who have visited areas at risk of outbreaks. A person who does not fall under the above cases but would like a screening test may avail himself or herself of the test, upon paying $142. This is about 5% of the total monthly average wage for Korean wage workers ($2,879.20, as of May 2019). In addition, patients with a "positive" diagnostic test result may receive a refund for the test cost.

(c)    Open Application Program Interface Service

In March 2020, HIRA opened the Open API data, which can provide information on COVID-19 National Safe Hospitals and Screening Centers through a public data portal. Using the information collected from the API, the MOHW discloses the state of operation of National Safe Hospitals and Screening Centers nationwide through the official website in real-time (https://www.mohw.go.kr/react/popup_200128.html). The main information disclosed includes clinics and operating hours by region, possible procedures, contact information, and location (including map service). It is also possible to search by integrating the administrative region, institution name, and phone number.

## Test Kit Development through Research and Development

In January 2020, as soon as the genetic sequences of COVID-19 were released, the Korean Society for Laboratory Medicine developed a reportable mass molecular genetic test method (RT-PCR), collaborating with the KCDC and the Korean Association of External Quality Assessment Service, that can quickly report accurate test results to meet the rapidly increasing demand for diagnostic tests for suspected COVID-19 patients. The new test method was a new genetic test that can be confirmed within 6 hours, unlike the existing "pan-corona test method," which takes 1 to 2 days.

After completing the verification of the new test method, KCDC disclosed it for the manufacture of diagnostic kits to domestic reagent manufacturing companies. The Ministry of Food and Drug Safety has conducted EUA for the kit, and it has been used by private medical institutions since February. The diagnostic reagents marketed with EUA in the ROK from February to June are products of seven companies (Table 4).

**Table 4: Features and Reading Standards of Seven Types of COVID-19 Diagnostic Kits Authorized by Emergency Use Authorization**

| EUA Assay | Company | Target Gene | Internal Control (IC) | Indicating COVID-19 | Approval Date |
|---|---|---|---|---|---|
| PowerCheck 2019-nCoV | Kogenbiotech, Seoul | E, RdRp | Recombinant plasmid DNA | E Ct ≤ 35 and RdRp Ct ≤ 35 | 4 Feb |
| Allplex 2019-nCoV | Seagene, Seoul | E, RdRp, N | Bacteriophage | E Ct ≤ 40, RdRp Ct ≤ 40, and N ≤ 40 | 12 Feb |
| Standard M nCoV Real-Time Detection | SD Biosensors, Suwon | N, ORFlab (RdRp) | Lentivirus | N Ct ≤ 36 and ORFlab Ct ≤ 36 | 27 Feb |
| DiaPlexQ 2019-nCoV | Solgent, Daejeon | N, ORFla | Rice phosphoglycerate kinase gene, mRNA | N Ct ≤ 40 or ORFla Ct ≤ 40 | 27 Feb |
| Real-Q 2019-nCoV | BioSewoom, Seoul | E, RdRp | Human RNase P gene (intrinsic) | E Ct ≤ 38 and RdRp Ct ≤ 38 | 13 Mar |
| BioCore 2019-nCoV Real Time PCR | BioCore, Seoul | N, RdRp | Human β-globin gene (intrinsic) | N Ct ≤ 40 and RdRp Ct ≤ 40 | 8 May |
| careGENE N-CoV RT-PCR | Wells Bio, Seoul | E, RdRp | – | E Ct ≤ 45 and RdRp Ct ≤ 45 | 28 May |

COVID-19 = coronavirus disease, EUA = Emergency Use Authorization.
Sources: H. Sung et al. 2020. COVID-19 molecular testing in Korea: Practical essentials and answers from experts based on experiences of emergency use authorization assays. *Ann Lab Med.* 40. pp. 439–47; Ministry of Food and Drug Safety. https://www.mfds.go.kr/brd/m_74/view.do?seq=43838&srchFr=&srchTo=&srchWord=&srchTp=&itm_seq_1=0&itm_seq_2=0&multi_itm_seq=0&company_cd=&company_nm=&page=1.

### Box 4: Real-Time Polymerase Chain Reaction Test

The in vitro diagnostic technology used in the real time polymerase chain reaction (RT-PCR) test is a molecular diagnostic technology, which is a diagnostic method based on information on human nucleic acids (DNA, RNA). It is a technology that amplifies the gene of the sample causing the disease to find a specific gene containing pathogen information and diagnoses whether it is infected. The test proceeds by collecting a patient sample (upper and lower respiratory tract) → gene extraction → gene amplification → result analysis). The diagnostic accuracy of molecular diagnostic technology has a sensitivity and specificity of more than 95%, and it takes about 6 hours to obtain a result after the test.

Source: Korea Health Industry Development Institute (KHIDI). 2020. COVID-19 Diagnostic Equipment Industry Status and Export Forecast. *KHIDI brief* 2020, 303.

## Implementation

The RT-PCR diagnostic method developed in the ROK was approved as an international standard (DIS) by the International Organization for Standardization/Technical Committee 212 (ISO/TC 212) in February, and is expected to be established as an international standard within the year after final approval by each member country.

In addition, according to the performance ranking of the COVID-19 Molecular Diagnosis Kit released by the Food and Drug Administration (FDA) on 15 September, two products by Korean companies were included among the top eight products. To accurately compare the performance between EUA authorized diagnostic kits, FDA delivered a standard sample and standard operating procedure directly to 154 molecular diagnostic kit developers around the world. After that, a blind test was conducted to compare Limit of Detection by receiving test results from each developer. The FDA has released a performance ranking of 55 COVID-19 molecular diagnostic kits from companies that have sent the results (Figure 10). Of a total 13 domestic companies that received approval for emergency use of the COVID-19 Diagnosis Kit by the FDA (Osang Healthcare, Seegene, SD Biosensor, Sight Biomaterials, Biocore, Optorane, LabGnomics, Gene Matrix, Gencurix, Access Bio, Bioseum, Kogen Biotech, Solgent), 10 companies sent the results.

By using self-developed diagnostic test methods, the ROK has built up the capability to perform 20,000 tests a day in early March. In addition, rapid diagnosis technology enables early diagnosis, leading to rapid isolation of confirmed cases and reduction of transmission.

### Figure 10: Performance of the Emergency Use Authorization COVID-19 Molecular Diagnostic Tests Using the Food and Drug Administration Reference Panel

| Product LoD (NDU/mL***) | Developer | Test |
|---|---|---|
| 180 | PerkinElmer, Inc. | PerkinElmer New Coronavirus Necleic Acid Detection Kit |
| 540 | ScienCell Research Laboratories | ScienCell SARS-CoV-2 Coronavirus Real-time RT-PCR (RT-qPCR) Detection Kit |
| 600 | BioCore Co., Ltd. | BioCore 2019-nCoV Real Time PCR Kit |
| 600 | DiaCarta, Inc. | QuantiVirus SARS-CoV-2 Test Kit |
| 600 | DiaCarta, Inc. | QuantiVirus SARS-CoV-2 Multiplex Test Kit |
| 600 | Hologic, Inc. | Panther Fusion SARS-CoV-2 Assay |
| 600 | Hologic, Inc. | Aptima SARS-CoV-2 Assay |
| 600 | SEASUN BIOMATERIALS | U-TOP COVID-19 Detection Kit |
| 1800 | Becton, Dickinson & Company (BD) | BioGX SARS-CoV-2 Reagents for BD MAX System |
| 1800 | CirrusDx Laboratories | CirrusDx SARS-CoV-2 Assay |
| 1800 | Euroimmun US, Inc. | EURORealTime SARS-Cov-2 |
| 1800 | Helix OpCo LLC(dba Helix) | Helix COVID-19 Test |
| 1800 | LabGenomics Co., Ltd. | LabGun COVID-19 RT-PCR Kit |
| 1800 | Quest Diagnostics Infectious Disease, Inc. | Quest SARS-CoV-2 rRT-PCR |
| 1800 | Rheonix, Inc. | Rheonix COVID-19 MDx Assay |
| 1800 | Roche Molecular Systems, Inc. (RMS) | cobas SARS-CoV-2 |
| 2500 | Applied DNA Sciences, Inc. | Linea COVID-19 Assay Kit |
| 3600 | Fulgent Therapeutics, LLC | Fulgent COVID-19 by RT-PCR Test |
| 5400 | Abbott Molecular | Abbott RealTime SARS-CoV-2 assay |
| 5400 | Access Bio, Inc. | CareStart COVID-19 MDx RT-PCR |
| 5400 | Applied BioCode, Inc. | BioCode SARS-CoV-2 Assay |
| 5400 | Assurance Scientific Laboratories | Assurance SARS-CoV-2 Panel |
| 5400 | Becton, Dickinson & Company | BD SARS-CoV-2 Reagents for BD MAX System |
| 5400 | BioFire Defense, LLC | BioFire COVID-19 Test |
| 5400 | Boston Heart Diagnostics | Boston Heart COVID-19 RT-PCR Test |

*continued on next page*

Figure 10 *continued*

| Product LoD (NDU/mL***) | Developer | Test |
|---|---|---|
| 5400 | Cepheid | Xpert Xpress SARS-CoV-2 Test |
| 5400 | ChromaCode Inc. | HDPCR SARS-CoV-2 Assay |
| 5400 | Ethos Laboratories | Ethos Laboratories SARS-CoV-2 MALDI-TOF Assay |
| 5400 | GeneMatrix, Inc | NeoPlex COVID-19 Detection Kit |
| 5400 | Hackensack University Medical Center (HUMC) Molecular Pathology Laboratory | CDI Enhanced COVID-19 Test |
| 5400 | KogeneBiotech Co., Ltd. | PowerChek 2019-nCov Real-time PCR Kit |
| 5400 | Luminex Molecular Diagnostics, Inc. | NxTAG CoV Extended Panel Assay |
| 5400 | Patients Choice Laboratories, LLC | PCL SARS-CoV-2 Real-Time RT-PCR Assay |
| 5700 | Centers for Disease Control and Prevention (CDC) | Influenza SARS-CoV-2(Flu SC2) Multiplex Assay |
| 6000 | DiaSorin Molecular LLC | Simplexa COVID-19 Direct assay |
| 6000 | Quidel Corporation | Lyra SARS-CoV-2 Assay |
| 6000 | Seasun Biomaterials, Inc. | AQ-TOP COVID-19 Rapid Detection Kit |
| 6000 | Sherlock BioSciences, Inc. | Sherlock CRISPR SARS-CoV-2 Kit |
| 6000 | University of North Carolina Medical Center | UNC Health SARS-CoV-2 real-time RT-PCR test |
| 6030 | Exact Sciences Laboratories | SARS-CoV-2(N gene detection) Test |
| 7200 | PrivaPath Diagnostics, Inc.**** | LetsGetChecked Coronavisus (COVID-19) Test |
| 18000 | Acupath Laboratories, Inc | Acupath COVID-19 Real-Time (RT-PCR) Assay |
| 18000 | Avellino Lab USA, Inc. | AvellinoCoV2 test |
| 18000 | Infectious Diseases Diagnostics Laboratory (IDDL), Boston Children's Hospital | Childrens-Altona-SARS-CoV-2 Assay |
| 18000 | Centers for Disease Control and Prevention (CDC) | CDC 2019-nCoV Real-Time RT-PCR Diagnstic Panel (CDC) |
| 18000 | Color Genomics, Inc.**** | Color Genomics SARS-CoV-2 RT-LAMP Diagnostic Assay |
| 18000 | Eli Lilly and Company | Lilly SARS-CoV-2 Assay |
| 18000 | Enzo Life Sciences, Inc. | AMPIPROBE SARS-CoC-2 Test System |
| 18000 | Gravity Diagnostics, LLC | Gravity Diagnostics COVID-19 Assay (370KB) |
| 18000 | HealthQuest Esoterics | HealthQuest Esoterics TaqPath SARS-CoV-2 Assay |
| 18000 | Pathology/Laboratory Medicine Lab of Baptist Hospital Miami | COVID-19 RT-PCR Test |
| 18000 | Psomagen, Inc. | Psoma COVID-19 RT Test |
| 180000 | Diatherix Eurofins Laboratory | SARS-CoV-2 PCR Test |
| 180000 | Luminex Corporation | ARIES SARS-CoV-2 Assay |
| 180000 | QIAGEN GmbH | QIAstat-Dx Respiratory SARS-CoV-2 Panel |

COVID-19 = coronavirus disease, NDU/ml: Nucleic acid amplification test-detectable units (NDU) per (ml) milliliter, RT-PCR = real-time polymerase chain reaction, SARS = severe acute respiratory syndrome.

Note: Companies and/or products by the Republic of Korea are marked in red boxes.

Source: Adapted from SARS-COV-2 Reference Panel Comparative Data.

# 3.2  Tracing

**KEY MESSAGE**

*Systematizing the epidemiological investigation process, training human resources, and investment have been conducted among the government, the Korea Centers for Disease Control and Prevention (KCDC), and local governments in the Republic of Korea (ROK). After the large-scale spread of COVID-19, computerization of the epidemiological investigation process has emerged for more efficient response to the crisis. Data related to personal movement provided by the Smart Management System to the epidemiological investigator include mobile phone location data; CCTV images; and details of use of cash cards, ATMs, and credit cards. The quarantine authorities have ordered to record the list of visitors for facilities with an unspecified number of people; a digital customer register system (KI-PASS) based on a quick response (QR) code was developed. Point-of-entry screening requires quarantine for 14 days for all inbound travelers from all countries around the world. All citizens of the ROK and long-stay foreigners should mandatorily install the "Self-quarantine Safety Protection App" and abide by the guidelines including submitting their health status on the Self-Diagnosis App for a period of 14 days. Also, if a person violates the quarantine guidelines, he or she is advised to wear a safety band for the remainder of their quarantine period.*

## Epidemiological Investigation Support System

The ROK suffered socioeconomic damage throughout the country during the MERS outbreak in 2015, and as a result, felt the importance of quarantine and epidemiological investigations to prevent the spread of infectious diseases from overseas. Since then, systematization of the epidemiological investigation process, training of human resources, and investment have been closely conducted between the government, the KCDC, and local governments.

### Guidelines

The main purpose of the epidemiological investigation is to quickly determine whether an infectious disease occurs, and to identify the source of infection and transmission process. According to the ROK's quarantine system, when a new infectious disease appears, the local government where the patient has the disease forms an immediate response team and takes charge of quarantine. The response team conducts epidemiological investigations of confirmed patients, contact management, and environmental management measures according to key steps.

**Table 5: Stages of Epidemiological Investigation and Main Work Contents at Each Stage**

| Stage | Main Contents |
|---|---|
| **Preliminaries** | • Immediate response team formation<br>• Collect confirmed cases and contacts information<br>• Identify the size of the infection, the course, and the movement after symptoms<br>• Immediate self-quarantine for contacted persons<br>• Diagnosis after report for PUI<br>• Securing data on facilities (users, environment, etc.)<br>• Notification of epidemiological investigation |

*continued on next page*

Table 5 *continued*

| Stage | Main Contents |
|---|---|
| **On-site response** | • Set measures, epidemiological investigation plans, and priorities through initial situation evaluation<br>• Division of duties<br>• Epidemiological investigation<br>• On-site control (temporary restriction of movement until appropriate disinfection measures, contact investigation and management, and waste management) |
| **Measure** | • Management of confirmed cases (removal of quarantine when the criteria are met)<br>• Self-isolation of contacts and active monitoring<br>• (If necessary) facility closure |
| **Situation report** | • Daily report of epidemiological investigation to public (once a day)<br>• Immediate report in case of death |

PUI = patient under investigation.
Source: Central Disease Control Headquarters. COVID-19 Response Guideline (for local governments), 9-2 edition. (20.08.20.)

## Implementation

(a)    COVID-19 Smart Management System

After the large-scale spread of COVID-19, the need for computerization of the epidemiological investigation process emerged due to the data-intensive work of epidemiological investigators and the resulting delay in quarantine activities. Accordingly, KCDC proposed to the government to establish a system to quickly and accurately conduct epidemiological investigations. Since previous epidemiological investigations were conducted by sending official documents, contacting via phone, and recording a handwritten note, it was difficult to conduct an investigation when a large-scale transmission occurred. As a result, the Ministry of Land, Infrastructure and Transport built the Smart Management System (SMS) (Figure 11) using the "smart city data processing platform technology," which was previously being researched and developed, and officially started operation on 26 March 2020.

This system provides a function to check the routes of confirmed cases and large-scale outbreak areas in real-time by using "big data" established in connection with 28 organizations including the Ministry of Land, Infrastructure and Transport; the Ministry of Science and Technology Information and Communication (MSIT); and KCDC.

Data related to personal movement provided by the system to the epidemiological investigator include mobile phone location data; CCTV images; and details of use of cash cards, ATMs, and credit cards. In addition, the movement of confirmed cases is automatically displayed on the map and provided to epidemiological investigators, so they can be used to find close contact.

By using this system, the speed and accuracy of information collection during the epidemiological investigation is achieved (Figure 12). Ultimately, SMS has changed the epidemiological investigation system so that the quarantine authorities can quickly respond to large-scale transmission of COVID-19. The identification of the route of the confirmed cases, which took about 24 hours before the use of SMS, was completed within 10 minutes. In addition, by converting the information records of epidemiological investigation subjects from handwritten to computerized, information exchange between institutions became possible in real-time. Because the system was built to ensure the speed and efficiency of epidemiological investigations, and access rights to the information collected by this system are limited to epidemiological investigators, it is not easy to use them for research purposes such as identifying the infection chain of COVID-19.

**Figure 11: Diagram of the COVID-19 Smart Management System**

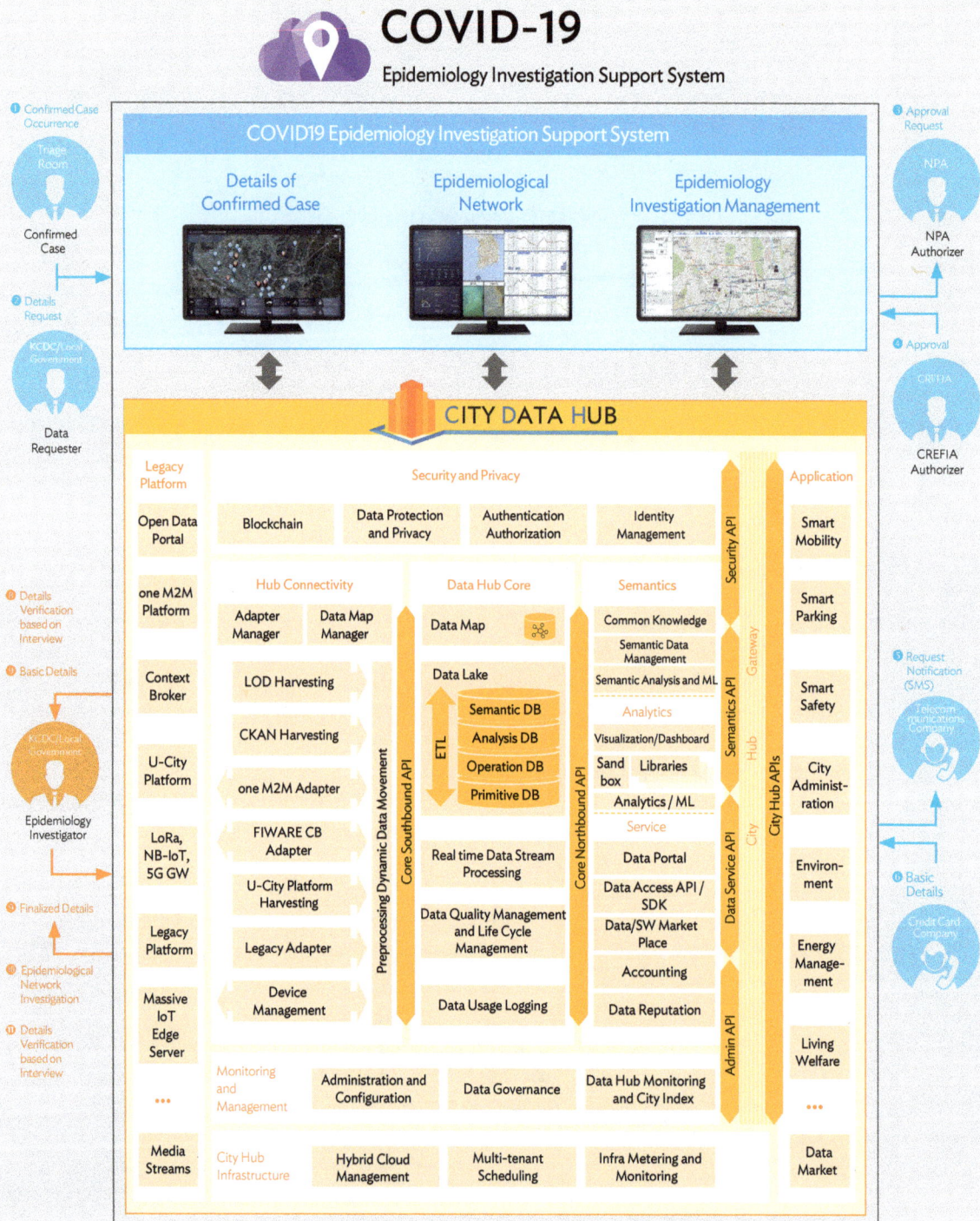

API = application program interface, CKAN = Comprehensive Knowledge Archive Network, COVID-19 = coronavirus disease, CREFIA = the Credit Finance Association, DB = database, GW = gigawatt, IoT = Internet of Things, KCDC = Korea Centers for Disease Control and Prevention, LOD = linked open data, ML = machine learning, NPA = National Policy Agency, SDK = software development kit, SMS = Smart Management System, SW = software.

Source: Adapted from "How We Fought COVID-19_A Perspective from Science and ICT."

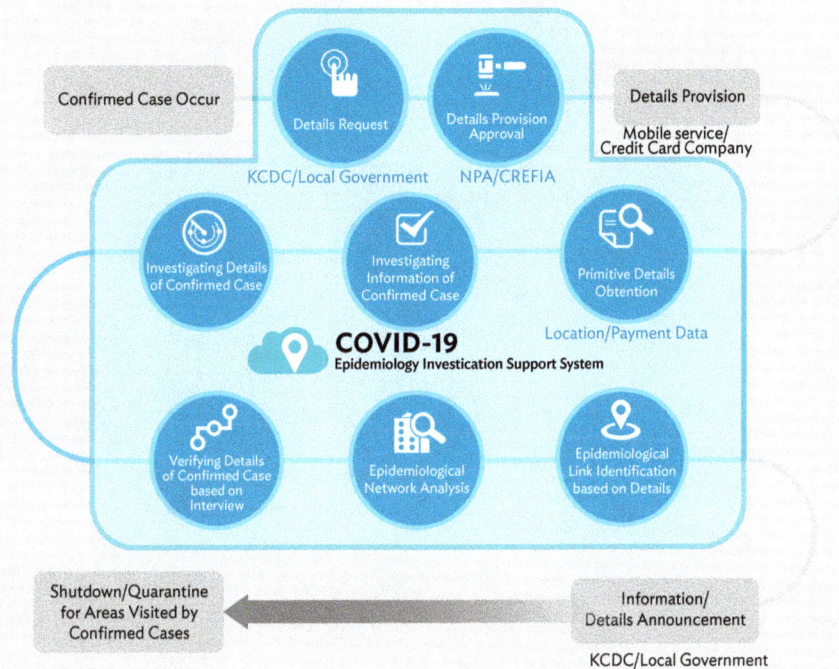

**Figure 12: Structure Supporting Epidemiological Investigation of the COVID-19 Smart Management System**

COVID-19 = coronavirus disease, CREFIA = the Credit Finance Association, KCDC = Korea Centers for Disease Control and Prevention, NPA: National Policy Agency.
Source: Adapted from "COVID-19 Smart Management System. Leveraging Data Hub developed under the Korean National Strategic Smart City Program (NSSC Program)."

(b)    KI-PASS (Korea Internet Pass)

Since the outbreak of COVID-19, several cases of mass transmissions occurred at facilities where multiple people gathered, and the quarantine authorities have ordered to record the list of visitors for facilities with an unspecified number of people from 22 March 2020. However, in an epidemiological investigation of mass transmissions in an entertainment facility in May, only 41% of the visitors on the list were able to make phone calls because the information was false. After that, for a quick and accurate epidemiological investigation of COVID-19, the MOHW developed a digital customer register system (KI-PASS) based on a QR code. The information that can be collected with the KI-PASS system and how to use it is as follows.

- Facility user - When using the facility, present the individual QR code issued through the QR-issuing company to the facility manager on the mobile phone.
- Facility manager - Install an app for facility managers and create visit records by scanning the facility user's QR code.
- QR-issuing company - Store and manage individual QR code information generated by the app in the server.
- Korea Social Security Information Service (KSSS) - Store and manage facility information and user visit information (QR code recognition record) collected in the server (MOHW).
- When a confirmed case occurs, quarantine authorities such as MOHW request and receive confirmed visitor information (KSSS) and personal information (QR code issuer) that were stored separately. Combined, personally identified information is used for epidemiological investigations.

The collected information is discarded after 30 days.

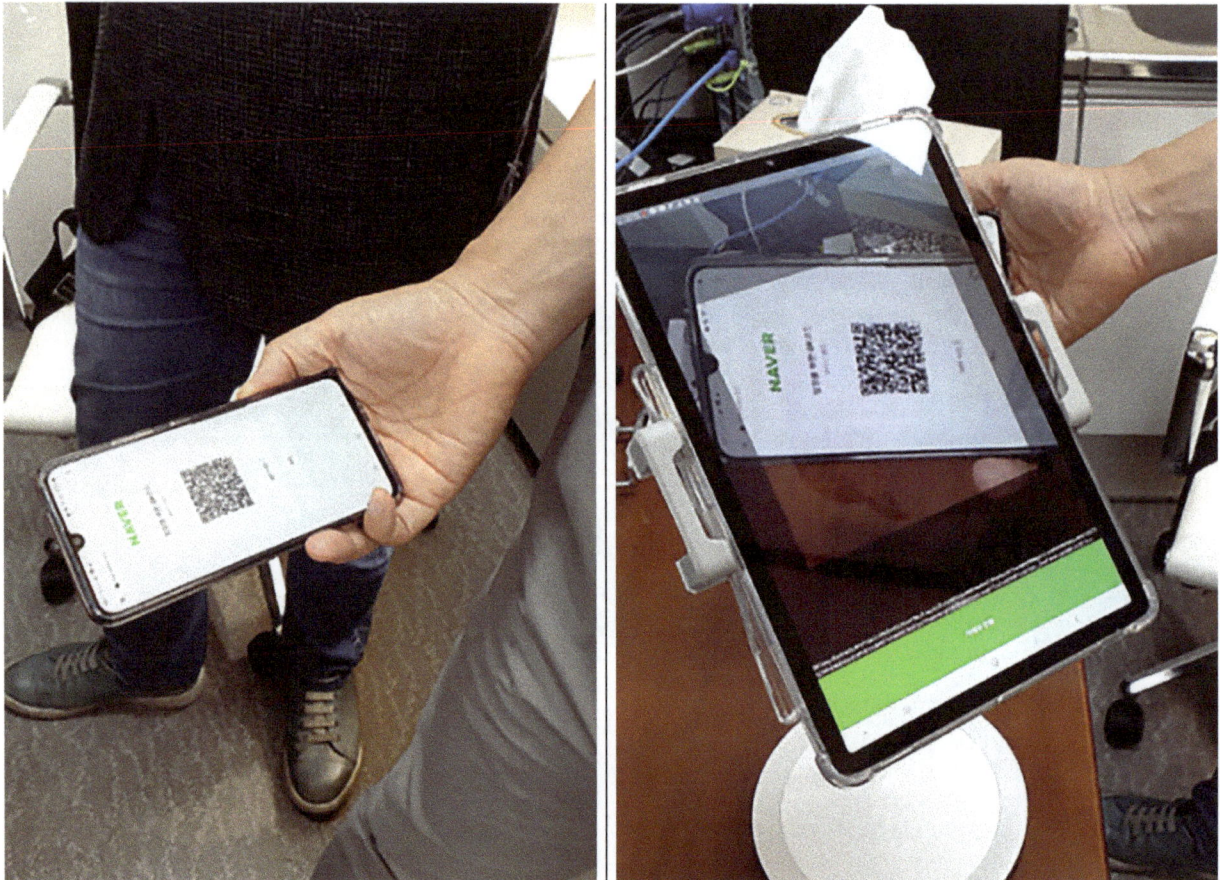

**Korea Internet Pass.** QR code issuance (left) and scanning (right) (Photo by Ministry of Health and Welfare).

## Point-of-Entry Screening

As the outbreak of COVID-19 around the world increases, the Government of the ROK has conducted quarantine for 14 days from 12 midnight on 1 April, for all inbound travelers from all countries around the world (Figure 13).

### Guidelines

(a)    Symptomatic Travelers

All travelers entering the ROK (both Korean and foreign nationals) are tested if they exhibit fever or respiratory symptom identified at entry screening. Travelers who test positive for COVID-19 are transferred to a hospital or residential treatment center. Korean nationals or foreign nationals on long-term visas who test negative are placed under self-quarantine (14 days, Self-Quarantine Safety Protection App to be installed) and foreign nationals on short-term visas are placed under quarantine at facilities (14 days, Self-Diagnosis App to be installed).

(b)    Asymptomatic Travelers

Asymptomatic Korean and foreign nationals from Europe and the United States (US) on long-term visas are subject to self-quarantine (14 days, Self-Quarantine Safety Protection App to be installed) and tested at a public health center within 3 days of arrival. Asymptomatic Korean nationals and foreign nationals on long-term visas from countries other than the US and European countries are subject to self-quarantine (14 days, Self-Quarantine Safety Protection App to be installed) and tested at a public health center within 14 days.

Asymptomatic foreign nationals from Europe and the US on short-term visas are subject to facility quarantine (14 days, Self-Quarantine Safety Protection App and Self-Diagnosis App to be installed). Asymptomatic foreign nationals from countries other than the US and European countries on short-term visas are subject to facility quarantine (14 days, Self-Diagnosis App to be installed) and tested at a public health clinic within 14 days.

**Figure 13: Protocol for National Entrants (Symptomatic Travelers, and Asymptomatic Korean Nationals and Foreign Nationals on Long-Term Visas)**

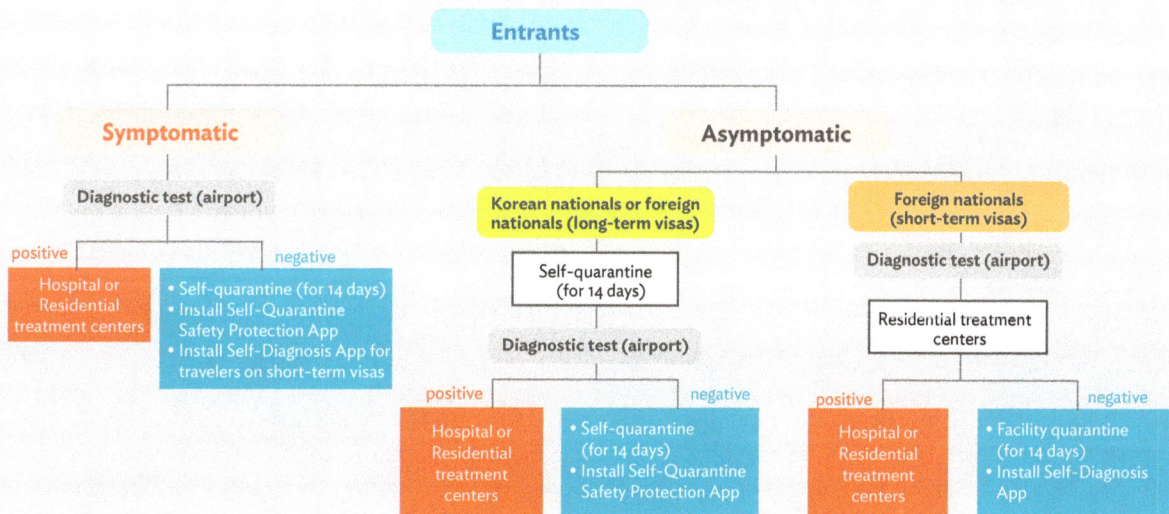

Source: Modified from a website operated by the Ministry of Health (http://ncov.mohw.go.kr/).

(c)    Travelers Exempt from Quarantine

Travelers holding A1 (Diplomat) or A2 (Government official) visas, or Quarantine Exemption Certificate issued by the Korean Embassy or Consulate General prior to the entry, receive tests and wait for the results at a temporary screening facility. If they test negative, they are subject to active monitoring for 14 days from the day of arrival by installing the Self-Diagnosis App of the MOHW.

**Implementation**

(a)    Safe Return Home Service

If Koreans who have entered the country from abroad and passed point-of-entry screening in the airport cannot use their own car, the local government operates special transportation to help them return home. This is to prevent the transmission of infection by asymptomatic infected individuals by minimizing contact with the local community of immigrants who are obligated to self-isolate for 14 days.

(b)    Penalty

If a traveler entering the ROK does not comply with the quarantine guidelines, he or she may face up to 1 year of imprisonment or a $9,000 fine for violating the Quarantine Act and Infectious Disease Control and Prevention Act. In accordance with the Immigration Act, foreign nationals violating the regulations may face deportation or ban on entry into the ROK.

## Self-Diagnosis and Self-Quarantine Applications

All Koreans and long-stay foreigners should mandatorily install the "Self-Quarantine Safety Protection App" (Figure 14) by the Ministry of the Interior and Safety and abide by the guidelines for self-quarantined persons including submitting their health status on the Self-Diagnosis App for 14 days. The app supports local self-quarantine monitoring tasks such as self-diagnosing the health status of self-quarantine, automatically notifying dedicated public officials, and sending a notification when leaving the quarantine site.

**Implementation**

(a)    Self-Quarantine Safety Protection App

The Self-Quarantine Safety Protection App (Figure 15) has the following main functions: (i) Self-quarantine information registration (Personal information, self-isolation location information, etc.); (ii) Self-diagnosis (Self-diagnosis alert, Submit the results) - A user needs to conduct self-diagnosis twice a day; (iii) Provision of safety information for self-quarantine (Living rules, how to use the app, etc.), (iv) Emergency contact (Phone number of a dedicated official, and KCDC); (v) Motion detection to check whether the smartphone is moving; and (vi) Relief band and smartphone connection status detection.

(b)    Self-Diagnosis Mobile App

People with A visas (Diplomat [A-1], Government Official [A-2]) or Quarantine Exemption Certificate issued by the Embassy of the ROK should install the Self-Check Mobile App and record their daily health status on the app for 14 days after arrival in the ROK. Personal details entered in the Self-Diagnosis App should coincide with the information submitted in the Travel Record Special Declaration. If there is a change to personal details, the person should update the information in the app. Those who have installed the app will receive a daily SMS notification to submit their daily health status for 14 days after entering the ROK.

## Figure 14: How to Install the Self-Quarantine Safety Protection App

**질병관리본부 KCDC** | **해외감염병 NOW** | **감염관리본부 ☆ 센터**

### Coronavirus Disease-19 ( COVID-19 )

# MANDATORY QUARANTINE INSTRUCTIONS
## FOR ALL INCOMING TRAVELERS TO REPUBLIC OF KOREA

In accordance with the Infectious Disease Control and Prevention Act, **all incoming travelers, regardless of nationality, shall be subject to mandatory 14-day quarantine** beginning on the date of entry and ending at 12:00 of the 15th day. (For example, if you arrived on 1 June, you are required to stay under mandatory quarantine until 12:00 of 15 June.) (*The exact time may differ in the case of facility quarantine and will be announced by the quarantine facility.)

## ONCE YOU ARRIVE AT AIRPORT

✅ Wear a facemask at all times and avoid contact or talking with other people.

✅ You are required to be tested if you have suspected symptoms.

✅ **FOREIGNERS ON SHORT-TERM VISIT** are required to enter mandatory quarantine (at their own expense) at a facility designated by the Korean government.
ALL INCOMING TRAVELERS (regardless of point of origin or nationality) are required to receive a COVID-19 test. For travelers entering through Incheon International Airport, you will get tested at an open walk-through screening station located at the airport during the hours 9:00-19:00 or at a temporary accommodation facility during 19:00-09:00.

✅ Note) Those who have valid quarantine exemption are required to be tested and will be subject to active monitoring for 14 days by designated public health officials. The designated official will check and monitor their health conditions for 14 days.
* Valid quarantine exemptions are:
   - Pre-approved waiver from the Ministry of Foreign Affairs; or
   - A1 (diplomat on duty) or A2 (government official on duty) visa or a "quarantine exemption document" issued in advance by a Korean Embassy.

✅ **FOREIGNERS ON LONG-TERM VISIT**
(i.e. living in Korea) are required to enter mandatory quarantine in their homes.

If you do not have symptoms at the time of entry, you may leave the airport and enter your mandatory home quarantine.
**However, you are required to visit a screening center and get tested within the next 3 days (i.e. during your home quarantine period), regardless of symptoms.**
*Further actions may follow contingent on test result.

✅ **FOR ALL PERSONS SUBJECT TO MANDATORY FACILITY QUARANTINE :**
- Use the designated transit vehicle to move to your designated quarantine facility.

JUNE 12, 2020

*continued on next page*

Figure 15 *continued*

질병관리본부 KCDC    해외감염병 NOW    1339

✓ **FOR ALL PERSONS SUBJECT TO MANDATORY HOME QUARANTINE :**
- When you leave the airport, do not take public transportation.
  Use a personal car or designated mode of transit (designated airport limousine bus or KTX train).
- Go home directly from the airport. Do not make stops in other locations.
- As soon as you arrive home, call your local public health center to inform them that you are under quarantine.
- Install the "HOME QUARANTINE SAFETY PROTECTION" app by the Ministry of the Interior and Safety on your phone. (This is mandatory.)

| Android | Google Play | App Store |
|---|---|---|
| [QR code] | [QR code] | [QR code] |
| http://url.kr/9dqRor | http://url.kr./5rntzH | http://url.kr/f7dmWs |

**ABOUT THE HOME QUARANTINE SAFETY PROTECTION APP :**
*All persons subject to mandatory home quarantine
(all Korean nationals and all foreign nationals on long-term visit)
are required to install the "HOME QUARANTINE SAFETY PROTECTION"
app on their mobile phone and comply with
the quarantine rules for 14 days of quarantine. (ID: CORONA)
(If there is any change to your phone number or where you live,
you must notify your local public health center as soon as possible.)

# HOME QUARANTINE GUIDELINES

✓ **INSTRUCTIONS FOR PERSON UNDER MANDATORY HOME QUARANTINE:**
- To protect other people in your community from possible infection, do not leave your quarantine location (i.e. your home) as much as possible.
- If you need to leave home for an essential need (such as getting medical care), contact your local public health center first.
- Make sure to secure an independent living space.
- If there is any space in your home that is shared with other household members (such as family members, roommates, and cohabitants),
  make sure that the common space is frequently ventilated.
- If you are unable to secure an independent living space, ask your local public health center for help.
- Keep your personal items (such as towels, eating utensils, and mobile phones) separate from other household members.
- Immediately report to your local public health center if you begin to show fever, cough, shortness of breath, or other respiratory symptoms.

✓ **INSTRUCTIONS FOR HOUSEHOLD MEMBERS LIVING WITH PERSON
UNDER MANDATORY HOME QUARANTINE:**
- To your best ability, avoid any physical contact with the quarantined household member.
- In situations where you have to come in contact with the quarantined household member, make sure to wear a facemask and
  keep a distance of at least 2 meters between you and the person.
- Closely monitor the health condition of the quarantined household member.
- Keep clean all frequently touched surfaces and objects including tabletops, door knobs, bathroom fixtures, bedside tables, and keyboards.
- If your work setting involves frequent contact with many people (including but not limited to school, private classes, preschool, kindergarten,
  social welfare facility, postpartum care center, and healthcare institution), limit or reduce your work capacity as best as possible to minimize
  contact with others until your household member is released from mandatory home quarantine.

# GENERAL INFECTION PREVENTION TIPS

✓ Wash your hands thoroughly with soap and running water for over 30 seconds.

✓ Cover your nose and mouth using your upper sleeve when coughing.

✓ Do not touch your eyes, nose, or mouth with unwashed hands.

✓ Frequently ventilate your rooms.

✓ Wear a facemask if you have fever or respiratory or respiratory symptoms,
  or when you visit hospitals, clinics, or pharmacies.

*If you leave your quarantine location without permission during your mandatory home quarantine
period or otherwise fail to comply with quarantine guidelines, you will be required to wear a Safety Band
(a location-tracking wristband that wirelessly connects to your phone's Home Quarantine Safety Protection App).
If you still refuse to comply, you will be ordered to quarantine at a designated facility at your own expense.

✕ **Failure to comply with this action may result in:**
- Criminal penalty of imprisonment up to 1 year or a fine up to 10 million won according to Article 79-3, subparagraphs
  3 through 5 of the Infectious Disease Control and Prevention Act;
- Civil damages in the event that your failure to comply constitutes violation of law and causes damage to the state due to
  further transmission of the infectious disease and/or additional measures of disease control/prevention; and/or
- (For foreign nationals) Revocation of visa or residence permit, deportation, and/or prohibition of entry
  according to the Immigration Act.

JUNE 12, 2020

Source: KCDA guide. http://ncov.mohw.go.kr/upload/ncov/file/202006/1592306715713__20200616202515.pdf.

**Figure 15: Screenshots of the Self-Quarantine Safety Protection App**

**Splash screen**

**Contact information for dedicated officials/KCDC**

**Self-diagnosis**

KCDC = Korea Centers for Disease Control and Prevention.
Note: App can be installed via Google Play Store at https://play.google.com/store/apps/details?id=kr.go.safekorea.sqsm&hl=ko&gl=US.
Source: Ministry of Health and Welfare.

## Safety Band for Self-Quarantine

On 27 April, the Central Disaster and Safety Countermeasure Headquarters announced that to prevent community transmission of COVID-19, self-quarantine management will be reinforced using information and communication technology (ICT). If a person notified of self-quarantine is found to have violated the quarantine guidelines, he or she is advised to wear a safety band (Figure 16) for the remainder of their quarantine period. If they refuse to wear the band, the quarantine authorities changed their quarantine location to a facility from home, and they bear the costs.

**Figure 16: Safety Band Wearing Promotional Leaflet Announced by the Ministry of the Interior and Security**

Source: Ministry of the Interior and Safety. https://www.ganghwa.go.kr/open_content/main/bbs/bbsMsgDetail.do;jsessionid=75DE22AE3B9ABBC6E1B8F393E2C1496C?msg_seq=159&bcd=covid&pgdiv=main&add1=01&pgno=58.

### Implementation

The safety band is a device that operates in conjunction with a Self-Quarantine Safety Protection App installed on a mobile phone using the Bluetooth function. If the safety band deviates from the self-isolation area by more than 20 meters, the distance between the band and the mobile phone is more than 20 meters, or the band is damaged or cut, the manager in charge is automatically notified. No evaluation for this safety band operation is performed.

## 3.3 Treatment

**KEY MESSAGE**

*The national security safe hospital is a facility where patients with respiratory diseases can receive treatment separately from other patients during the entire treatment process. Life treatment centers are public facilities to manage patients with mild COVID-19 who do not require inpatient treatment. The facility can be a cost-effective and efficient alternative under the COVID-19 pandemic, in that it relieves severe medical resource shortages that prevent severely ill people from being hospitalized and can utilize facilities that already exist in the community.*

### National Safe Hospital

To establish a hospital system where citizens who visit medical institutions can receive treatment without fear of COVID-19 infection, the MOHW has designated and operated a national security safe hospital. The national security safe hospital is a facility where patients with respiratory diseases can receive treatment separately from other patients during the entire treatment process, from visits to discharge. The national security safe hospital must have adequate qualifications in terms of size, structure, and operation, and is managed by the MOHW and the Korean Hospital Association. Depending on the status of COVID-19 and changes in management policies, the qualifications of the national security safe hospital may change, and it is a principle to operate temporarily according to the COVID-19 situation. It is classified into type A and type B according to the presence or absence of screening clinics and inpatient facilities.

### Guidelines

(a)   Treatment Model

To prevent and manage the outbreak of COVID-19 infection in the hospital, the national safety hospital operates a dedicated treatment zone for respiratory diseases separated from non-respiratory diseases (Figure 17).

After confirming the presence of respiratory symptoms, all patients before entering the hospital are classified into (i) case definition (Confirmed Case, Suspected Case, and PUI); (ii) respiratory patients; and (iii) non-respiratory patients. At this time, the medical staff must check the DUR/ITS information. After patient classification, respiratory patients and non-respiratory patients can be treated separately. The special treatment area for respiratory patients is completely separate from the general patient so that the spread of infection in the hospital can be prevented in advance. Case definition subjects are to be quarantined or diagnosed according to the guidelines, and patients with pneumonia of unknown cause who need hospitalization will be quarantined separately.

## Figure 17: Treatment Flowchart of Patients Visiting the National Safe Hospital

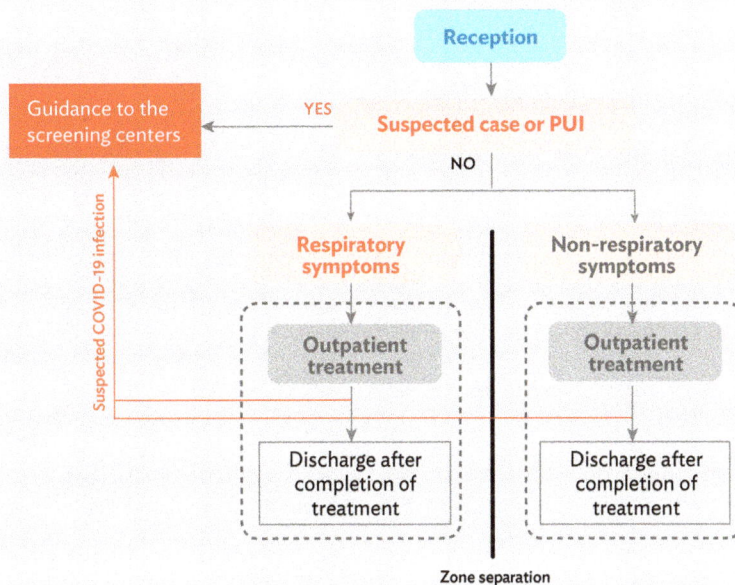

COVID-19 = coronavirus disease, PUI – patient under investigation.
Source: Ministry of Health and Welfare, Operating guideline for National Safe Hospital (3 March 2020). https://www.hira.or.kr/bbsDummy.do?pgmid=HIRAA020002000100&brdScnBltNo=4&brdBltNo=7816.

(b)    Infection Prevention Activities

In the hospitalization room and emergency room, visitors other than the guardian are completely controlled, and only one guardian who has gone through procedures can enter. In addition, guardians who are permitted to enter must observe infection prevention rules such as handwashing and coughing etiquette.

All medical staff must wear a mask in the hospital. In the case of ward treatment, personal protective equipment should be completed, and the possibility of infection to other wards should be blocked through thorough hygiene management. In addition, medical waste must be safely managed, and complete disinfection of hospital rooms, treatment rooms, operating rooms, and treatment equipment.

Several measures are needed to strengthen infection control in medical institutions. First, hygiene products such as hand sanitizer and disposable masks should be stocked throughout the institution. Second, a dedicated infection control team should be established to train employees, provide guidelines for infection prevention, and manage environmental improvement. Next, a rapid response team is formed to promptly quarantine and transfer patients, internal epidemiological investigations, and protect patients when a confirmed patient of COVID-19 occurs in the national safe hospitals. Lastly, countermeasures are taken in case of a confirmed COVID-19 case as an internal guideline and to educate the medical staff and employee to be familiar with them.

## Life Treatment Center

Life treatment centers are public facilities to manage patients with mild COVID-19 who do not require inpatient treatment. Medical staff and support personnel reside in the facility 24 hours a day, and provide medical care, living support, and quarantine. Residents self-monitor their body temperature and respiratory symptoms twice daily, and in case of an emergency, they can be transferred to the hospital at the discretion of the medical staff.

The center starts or ends flexibly according to the condition of the hospital bed in the area where the number of confirmed patients is increasing rapidly. It is mainly operated by utilizing facilities such as education and training centers owned by the government or corporations, university dormitories, or hotels.

## Guideline

At the life treatment center, patients could be discharged if they had no fever or clinical symptoms 7 days after the diagnosis, and two consecutive tests were negative at 24-hour intervals (Table 6). In addition, if at least one of the two diagnostic tests shows positive or undetermined results, retesting is performed after 7 days, and discharge is possible after two consecutive negative tests at 24-hour intervals. However, on 24 June 2020, as the criteria for quarantine for COVID-19 patients were eased, the conditions for dismissal at the life treatment center also changed. According to the revised criteria, discharge was possible if one of the clinical progress and PCR test results are met.

### Table 6: Conditions for Release of Quarantine in Asymptomatic COVID-19 Confirmed Patients

| Before 24 June 2020 | Revised on 24 June 2020 |
|---|---|
| Two consecutive negative test results at 24-hour intervals after 7 days from the date of diagnosis | 10 days after diagnosis, with no clinical symptoms occurring during that period. |
| AND | OR |
| If the PCR test result is positive on the seventh day after confirmation, two consecutive negative tests at 24-hour intervals | Two consecutive negative test results at 24-hour intervals after 7 days from the date of diagnosis |

COVID-19 = coronavirus disease, PCR = Polymerase Chain Reaction.
Source: Central Disease Control Headquarters. Central Disaster Management Headquarters. COVID-19 Response Guideline (for local governments), 9th edition. (20.06.25.)

### Figure 18: Illustration of Gyeongbuk-Daegu 7 Life Treatment Center

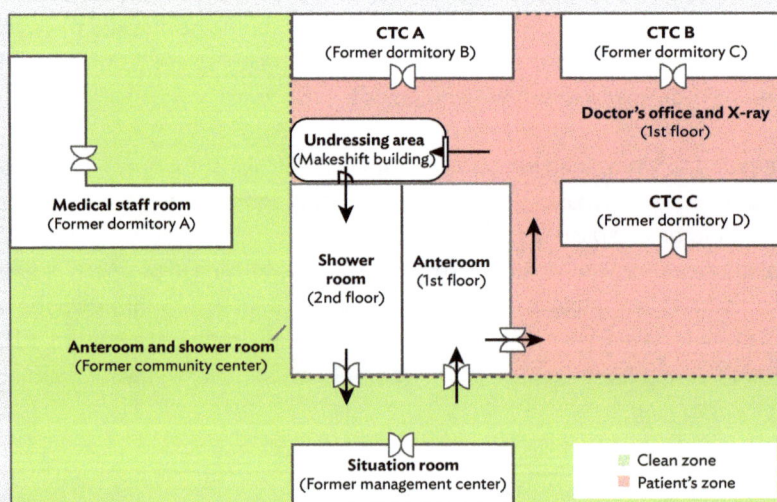

CTC = Community Treatment Center.
Note: Arrows indicate the movement direction of health-care providers.
Source: Adopted from Park et al. (2020).

Looking at the results of the initial 2 weeks of operation announced by the Gyeongbuk-Daegu 7 Life Treatment Center (Figure 18), one of the largest life treatment centers in the ROK, of a total of 309 patients who were initially admitted to the life treatment center, 7 patients were transported to the hospital due to worsening symptoms during the first 2 weeks, and 107 patients were discharged without complications. There was no case of a patient with a mild condition that worsened being hospitalized, and no cases of cross-infection of health-care providers were reported. The life treatment center can be a cost-effective and efficient alternative under the COVID-19 pandemic, in that it relieves severe medical resource shortages that prevent severely ill people from being hospitalized and can utilize facilities that already exist in the community.

### Figure 19: Scope of K-Quarantine International Standardization (Testing, Tracking, and Treatment)

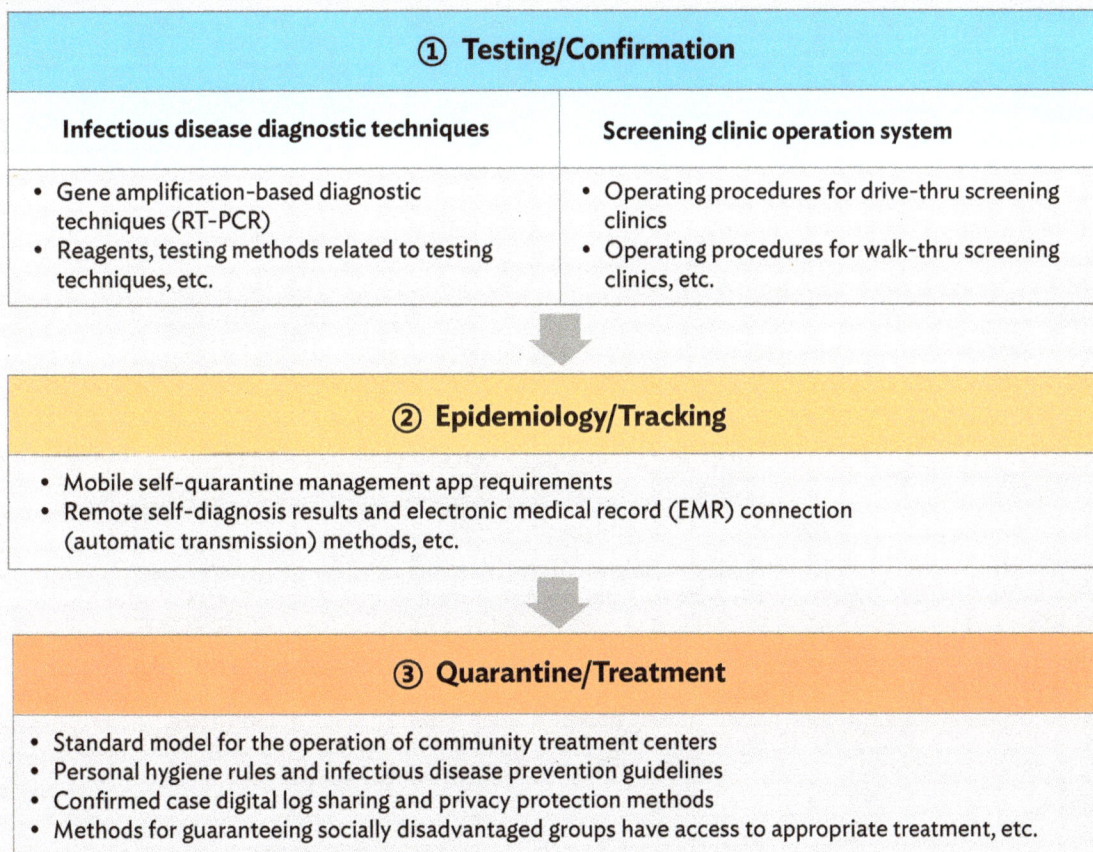

**① Testing/Confirmation**

| Infectious disease diagnostic techniques | Screening clinic operation system |
|---|---|
| • Gene amplification-based diagnostic techniques (RT-PCR)<br>• Reagents, testing methods related to testing techniques, etc. | • Operating procedures for drive-thru screening clinics<br>• Operating procedures for walk-thru screening clinics, etc. |

**② Epidemiology/Tracking**

• Mobile self-quarantine management app requirements
• Remote self-diagnosis results and electronic medical record (EMR) connection (automatic transmission) methods, etc.

**③ Quarantine/Treatment**

• Standard model for the operation of community treatment centers
• Personal hygiene rules and infectious disease prevention guidelines
• Confirmed case digital log sharing and privacy protection methods
• Methods for guaranteeing socially disadvantaged groups have access to appropriate treatment, etc.

EMR = electronic medical record, RT-PCR = real-time polymerase chain reaction.
Source: Ministry of Trade, Industry and Energy.

**Table 7: Response to COVID-19: 18 Measures for Testing, Tracking, and Treatment**

| 1. Testing/Confirmation | |
| --- | --- |
| | **Response to COVID-19** |
| **Infectious disease diagnostic technique** | • Reverse transcription polymerase chain reaction (RT-PCR) |
| | • Diagnostic reagent, equipment and test method |
| **Screening station management system** | • Drive-through screening station operation process |
| | • Walk-through screening standardized operation process |
| | • Mobile negative pressure container screening station standardized operation process |
| | • Screening station bidirectional test booth function and quality assessment standard |

| 2. Epidemiology/Tracking | |
| --- | --- |
| | **Response to COVID-19** |
| **Self-check quarantine management** | • Mobile self-check application requirements |
| | • Mobile self-quarantine application requirements |
| **Management system** | • Self-diagnosis/interview results and electronic medical record (EMR) linkage method |
| | • Function of the epidemiological investigation support system and personal information protection method |

| 3. Quarantine/Treatment | |
| --- | --- |
| | **Response to COVID-19** |
| **Quarantine** | • Operational guidelines for special immigration procedures to block the spread of infectious diseases between countries |
| | • Guidelines for preventing infectious disease cross-infection |
| | • Guidelines for personal hygiene management and social distancing in an infectious disease pandemic |
| | • Guidelines for essential social welfare services and medical support for vulnerable social groups in the event of an infectious disease disaster |
| **Treatment** | • Standard model for the operation of community treatment centers |
| | • Approval and follow-up evaluation of emergency use of in vitro diagnostic devices in the event of an infectious disease disaster |
| | • Classification of patients according to infectious disease symptoms and guidelines for management and operation of wards |
| | • Inventory/distribution/logistics management platform requirements for infectious disease essential diagnostic devices/medicine/anti-quarantine products/personal protective equipment (PPE) |

COVID-19 = coronavirus disease.
Source: Ministry of Health and Welfare. http://ncov.mohw.go.kr/tcmBoardView.do?contSeq=354963

# 3.4 Risk Communication during the COVID-19 Pandemic

**KEY MESSAGE**

*In addition to the daily briefing by the Central Disease Control Headquarters, the confirmed cases of COVID-19 that the public needs to know to prevent infection is promptly disclosed at the Ministry of Health and Welfare website, and through communications networks and press releases. Cell broadcasting service delivers emergency disaster information in real-time to mobile phones in the area in case of a disaster or crisis. Since the Korea Centers for Disease Control and Prevention provides data on the movement of COVID-19 confirmed cases to the application open interface (API), many developers voluntarily introduced a technical service that visualizes the information of confirmed cases on a map.*

## Daily Briefing

The Central Disease Control Headquarters announces information on the COVID-19 outbreak every day at 10 a.m. (24 hours from 12 midnight on the day). The contents of the announcement include regional and national statistics on the number of confirmed patients, deaths, diagnostic tests, and release from quarantine. In addition, information on the occurrence of new confirmed cases is disclosed to protect the privacy of patients and at the same time guarantee the public's right to know as much as possible.

## Disclosure Information on Routes of Confirmed Patients

In the event of a confirmed case of COVID-19, the information that the public needs to know to prevent infection is promptly disclosed by the MOHW website, communications network, and press releases. The scope of the information disclosed are (i) routes from 2 days before the onset of symptoms of the confirmed patient to the date of quarantine; and (ii) the patient's route of movement, transportation, medical institutions treated and contacts, etc. It is a principle not to disclose information specific to an individual such as gender, age, nationality, place of residence and company name., and if all contacts are identified, the space will not be disclosed.

**Table 8: Example of Disclosure Information on Routes of COVID-19 Confirmed Cases**

| Province | City | Type of place | Business Name (Address) | Date of Exposure | Disinfection |
|---|---|---|---|---|---|
| ○○ | ○○ | shop | ○○ market | 29 June (Mon), 13:00~15:00 | complete |
| ○○ | ○○ | public transport | ○○ bus | 30 June (Tues), 13:00~13:20 | expected |

○○ = unspecified name, date, etc., COVID-19 = coronavirus disease.

Source: Ministry of Health and Welfare. http://ncov.mohw.go.kr/bdBoardList_Real.do?brdId=1&brdGubun=12&ncvContSeq=&contSeq=&board_id=&gubun=.

**Figure 20: Disclosure Information on Routes of COVID-19 Confirmed Cases**

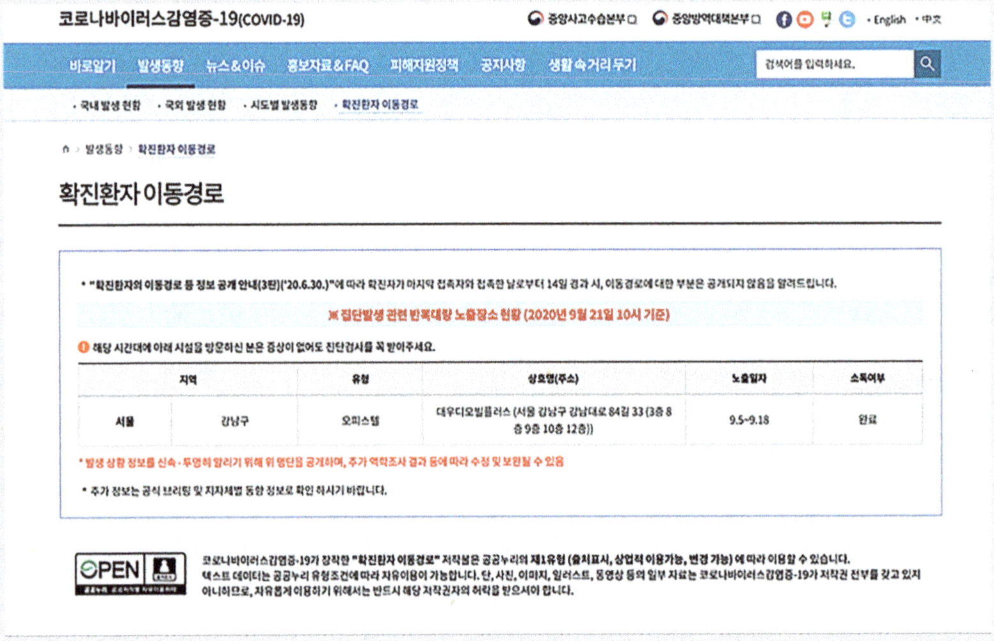

Source: Ministry of Health and Welfare.

## Safety Guidance Text Messages

The Ministry of Public Safety and Security implements the cell broadcasting service, which delivers emergency disaster information in real-time to mobile phones in the area in case of a disaster or crisis. By utilizing technology that can transmit data to all terminals in the same mobile communication base station at the same time, it provides the information of each region to the public in real-time under the COVID-19 crisis. The main contents of the disaster message are information on the occurrence of the confirmed case in the area where the base station is located, the main movement of the confirmed person, and high-risk facilities.

In addition, safety guidance text messages can be provided in English or Chinese by the "emergency disaster text foreign language translation service system" jointly developed by the Ministry of Public Administration and Security  and the Korea Tourism Organization. This is a

**Figure 21: Screenshot of the Emergency Ready App**

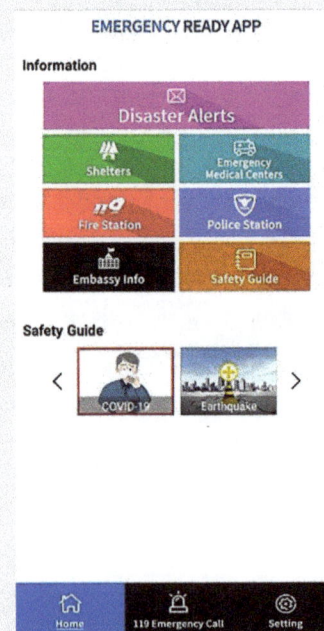

Source: Ministry of the Interior and Safety. https://www.mois.go.kr/frt/a02/localGovernmentArticle.do?dicaryinfoid=DICARY_0000000001970.

measure for the safety management of foreigners residing in the ROK and is provided by Emergency Ready App (Figure 21). App users can be alerted to the latest news related to COVID-19, and can also search for information on emergency shelters, emergency medical centers, fire stations, police stations, and safety guides.

## COVID-19 Maps to Geo-enable the Surveillance Information

The KCDC provides data on the movement of COVID-19 confirmed cases to the open API, which is updated daily. Based on this public data, many developers voluntarily introduced a technical service that provides integrated information to the public. In particular, services that visualize the information of confirmed cases on a map are widely used by the public. In addition, the following services are provided depending on the developer: (i) a warning alarm sounds when the person approaches the path within 100 meters (Coback), (ii) provides information on the number of contacts at the point set on the map (Corona Map), and (iii) displays information on the hospitals where the confirmed person is admitted and screening centers on the map (Corona Doctor).

# 4 Economic and Social Response

## 4.1 Economic Recovery: Public Sector

*To overcome the economic crisis and prepare for the post-COVID-19 economy, the Republic of Korea has passed four supplementary budgets. The budget usage is divided largely into four sections: revenue adjustment, financial support packages, strengthening employment and social safety nets, and financial stimulus packages. The Korean New Deal is the main policy of the financial stimulus packages. The government will invest a total of W31.3 trillion by 2022 to prepare for post-COVID-19.*

The Government of the Republic of Korea (ROK) is trying to directly support people's lives by approving four supplementary budget proposals. The first supplementary budget proposal of 2020 was approved on 17 March. The budget was worth about W11.7 trillion ($9.44 billion), with W2.1 trillion to be spent on disease prevention and treatment, W4.1 trillion to be spent on small business loans, W3.5 trillion to be spent on support for households including day care vouchers and emergency livelihood support, and W1.2 trillion won to be spent on local economies that were severely impacted (Ministry of Economy and Finance 2020a). The second supplementary budget worth W12.2 trillion, was passed at the National Assembly on 30 April. The supplementary budget was used to finance the household emergency relief program of up to W1 million for each household (Ministry of Economy and Finance 2020b).

Until the second supplementary budget, a total of W240 trillion was planned to be spent to boost the economy. The government has spent W150 trillion responding to COVID-19 through the Fourth National Economic Council Emergency Meetings: W32 trillion for stimulating the real economy, W100 trillion for avoiding financial market volatility, and W20 trillion for additional measures such as social security contribution support and emergency relief efforts. An additional W90 trillion was provided through the Fifth National Economic Council Emergency, which mentioned the possibility of a third supplementary budget. A total of W90 trillion was to be spent on employment (W10 trillion), key industries (W40 trillion), packages for people's livelihoods and financial stability (W35 trillion), and emergency loans for small business owners (W4.4 trillion).

The Assembly of the Republic of Korea approved the third supplementary budget worth W35.1 trillion on 3 July, which was the first time since 1972 that three supplementary budgets have been approved in a single year. The budget was proposed to overcome the economic crisis and prepare for the post-COVID-19 economy. This marks the biggest of the four supplementary budgets that the ROK has passed to contain COVID-19 and alleviate the economic slowdown caused by the continuing pandemic. The budget usage is divided largely into four sections: revenue adjustment, financial support packages, strengthening employment and social safety nets, and financial stimulus packages. About W11.4 trillion was used for making a revenue adjustment and support tax deductions. A total of W5 trillion from the third supplementary budget was used for financial support packages, which consist of second support measures for small businesses, emergency financing for SMEs, and emergency liquidity support for key industries and companies. A total of W10 trillion was used to strengthen employment and social safety nets. The budget was used to support emergency employment measures by expanding employee retention support, launching emergency employment stability subsidy, creating over 550,000 jobs in the public sector, and providing unemployment benefits. The budget was also used to expand social safety nets for low-income and vulnerable groups by expanding emergency welfare benefits; increasing microcredit for young adults; and providing affordable housing for families with multiple children, for young adults, and for newlyweds. Approximately W10.4 trillion was used for finance stimulus packages. Finance stimulus packages are split into three categories: (i) boosting domestic demand, exports, and local economies; (ii) the Korean New Deal; and (iii) the K COVID-19 response model and disaster management. To revitalize domestic demand, exports, and local economies, the government devised measures such as expanding local market gift certificates, promoting reshoring, and providing recovery support for SMEs and small businesses. The Korean New Deal is the main policy of the finance stimulus packages. The government will invest a total of W31.3 trillion by 2022 to prepare for post-COVID-19, and the third supplementary budget is used as the starting point of the Korean New Deal. About W4.8 trillion is allocated for the Korean New Deal which is over 45% of the finance stimulus packages budget. The Korean New Deal is composed of the Digital New Deal (Table 9), the Green New Deal, and the strengthening of employment security aimed at digital and green transformation and strengthening the social safety net. The Digital New Deal is a strategy to accelerate digital transformation triggered by COVID-19. It is largely composed of 12 tasks in 4 major areas. Lastly, W2.4 trillion is used to raise the K COVID-19 response model and disaster management to a global standard and strengthen the disaster response system (Ministry of Economy and Finance 2020c and 2020d).

### Table 9: Four Areas and 12 Tasks of the Digital New Deal

| Strengthening the Data-Network-A (D.N.A.) ecosystem | Digital Transformation of Education Infrastructure | Fostering the Un-Tact Industry | Social Overhead Capital Digitalization |
|---|---|---|---|
| • Data construction, opening, and utilization Spreading<br>• 5G·Artificial Intelligence (AI) convergence in all industries<br>• Intelligent government based on 5G/AI<br>• K-Cyber Prevention System | • A digital-based educational infrastructure for elementary, middle, and high schools<br>• Strengthening online education at universities and vocational training institutions nationwide | • Smart medical care and infrastructure<br>• Spreading remote work for small and medium-sized businesses<br>• Online business support for small enterprise | • Establishment of digital management system for core infrastructure in 4 areas<br>• Digital innovation in urban and industrial spaces<br>• Build a smart logistics system |

Source: Government of the Republic of Korea. Korean New Deal: National Strategy for a Great Transformation. https://english.moef.go.kr/pc/selectTbPressCenterDtl.do?boardCd=N0001&seq=4948.

Until the third supplementary budget, the government had prepared a policy package worth a total of W277 trillion through the first to eighth National Economic Council Emergency Meetings and three supplementary budgets. It includes W135 trillion in packages for people's livelihoods and financial stability, W40 trillion in basic industrial stabilization funds, and W46 trillion in additional reinforcement measures such as emergency disaster support funds. And now with the fourth supplementary budget confirmation, the government's direct support measures has increased to W285 trillion (Korea Development Institute [KDI] 2020).

## Figure 22: Growth Forecasts by Economic Outlook Scenarios

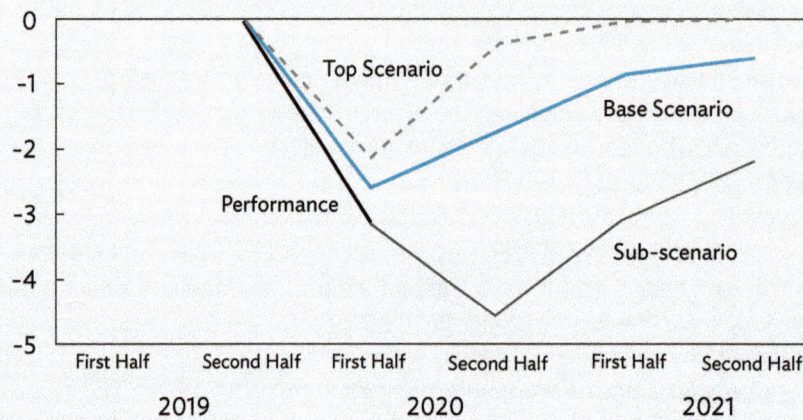

Source: Korea Development Institute, 2020

The economy was expected to recover to some extent by the end of 2020 through the massive third supplementary budget (Figure 22). However, the fourth supplementary budget proposal was inevitable due to the re-proliferation of COVID-19 in mid-August. Looking at the recent spread of COVID-19 in the ROK, it is similar to the "sub-scenario," in which the growth rate in the second half of the year is lower than in the first half, as the spread is rather stronger in the second half.

Therefore, the Korea Development Institute (KDI) has officially recognized a "reverse growth" by lowering its economic growth forecast for the ROK this year from 0.2% to –1.1% in its revised economic forecast (Figure 23). The KDI releases its economic forecast in May and November every year, but it is the third time that the revised forecast has been issued in the middle of the year, first after the 2009 global financial crisis (revised forecasts issued in January and September) and second in 2012 when the eurozone fiscal crisis took place (revised forecast issued in September). The government also hinted at the possibility of negative growth, saying that it is not easy

## Figure 23: Revision of Economic Forecast

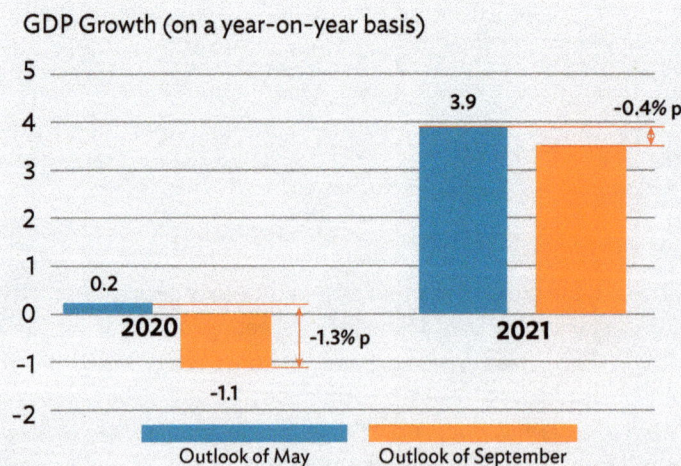

GDP = gross domestic product.
Source: Korea Development Institute, 2020.

to achieve this year's growth goal (0.1%), which was announced in June, considering the possibility of a delay in the pace of the economic rebound due to the re-proliferation of COVID-19 (KDI 2020).

According to the result of the Eighth Emergency Economic Council Meeting, a total of W12.4 trillion worth of relief funds will be provided, W7.8 trillion of which will be financed by the fourth supplementary budget, which was passed at the National Assembly on 22 September. The fourth supplementary budget will be spent mostly on COVID-19 relief, including small business support, unemployment support, childcare support, and emergency relief for low-income households. This means providing more support where necessary. It is focused rather than selective, and customized support rather than discriminatory.

On emergency relief for small businesses, the government decided to relieve the cash flow problems of small business by providing 2.91 million small business owners with a total of W3.2 trillion. The government plans to provide W500,000 per person to encourage small business owners to reenter the market. As COVID-19 special credit loans, the government will lower the interest rate for service SMEs, ventures, and exporters, and provide an additional W2.5 trillion in support. The tax breaks for cutting rents are extended until the end of 2020.

For emergency relief for contract workers and job seekers, the government decided to provide cash support for independent contractors worth W556 billion as additional secondary emergency employment stabilization measure.

The government will provide W400 billion for 890,000 people who are not supported by the existing livelihood support system or emergency support measures, despite suffering reduced income due to sudden job losses or shutdown.

Lastly, for emergency childcare support and others, the government will inject W2.2 trillion for parents who are facing the growing burden of childcare as day care centers and schools are closed or conducting classes remotely due to the re-proliferation of COVID-19. Also, it was decided to reduce the telecommunication fee by W20,000 for all Koreans (46.4 million people) who are 13 years old or older to relieve the burden of the non-contact and online era (Ministry of Economy and Finance 2020e). In addition to the fourth supplementary budget, there are W4.6 trillion worth of measures to support disease prevention and economic reinforcement that the administration wants to pursue through its own efforts. For the economic reinforcement, the administration allocated about W4 trillion to increase public spending by reducing unspent budgets and through early investment. Measures to boost the economy regarding Chuseok holiday have also been finalized. The administration decided to temporarily alleviate anticorruption laws to allow gifts worth up to W200,000 for farm and fishery products, an increase from W100,000. In addition, the administration decided to increase the supply of farm products that have high demand near the holidays and promote traditional market gift certificates (Ministry of Economy and Finance 2020e).

Despite these efforts, a V-shaped rebound seems far from reality due to the re-expansion of COVID-19 cases in August. Still, the economic growth of the ROK is somewhat better compared to other countries. The Organisation for Economic Co-operation and Development (OECD) released its *Interim Economic Outlook* on 16 September. Based on the outlook (Figure 24), the ROK's economic growth forecast by the OECD ranked first among the 37 OECD member countries. Among G20 countries, the ROK ranked second after the People's Republic of China, which is the only country expected to experience positive growth (1.8%) (OECD 2020).

According to the KDI report released on 8 September 2020, the ROK's economic outlook for 2021 is lower than the May forecast (3.5%–3.9%), but it is expected to show signs of recovery. Exports are expected to see a partial recovery, rising 3.4% in 2021, after falling 4.2% in 2020. Imports are expected to rise 3.7% in 2021 after recording a 4.2% decline due to sluggish domestic demand and exports in 2020. Although exports of services, as well as goods, stagnated in the first half of 2020 due to the spread of COVID-19, exports from the ROK are expected to

**Figure 24: OECD Economic Outlook Forecasts (September 2020)**

Real GDP Growth, on a year-on-year % Change

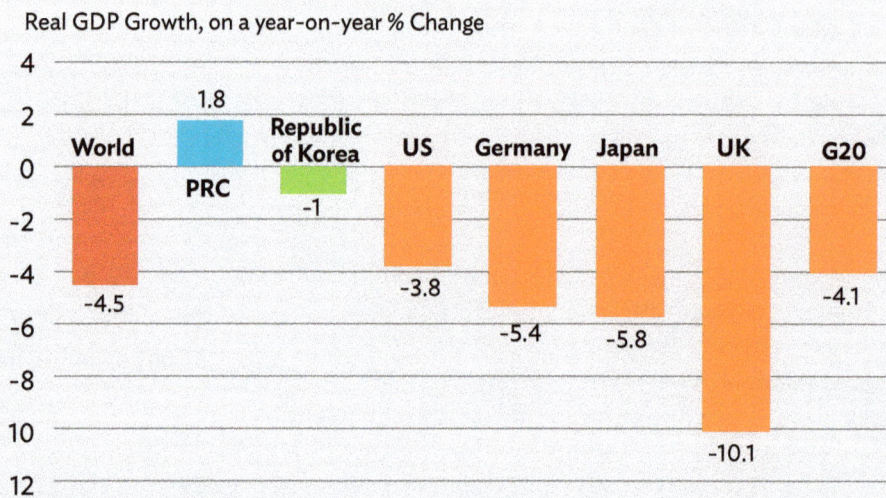

GDP = gross domestic product, OECD = Organisation for Economic Co-operation and Development, PRC = People's Republic of China, UK = United Kingdom, US = United States.
Source: OECD, 2020.

gradually rise as the global economy slowly moves out of recession due to large-scale stimulus policies by major countries. The current account balance is expected to post a surplus of $57 billion in 2020 as exports shrink due to the global economic recession, and a surplus of $58 billion in 2021, a slight rebound. Consumer prices are expected to rise 0.7% in 2021 as the economy and oil prices rally after recording a 0.5% low rise in 2020 as oil prices also fell sharply amid low-demand pressure due to the economic contraction. The number of employed people is expected to fall by 150,000 in 2020 as the job market shrinks, and then increase by 150,000 in 2021 after the economic slump eases (KDI 2020).

# 4.2  Economic Recovery: Private Sector

*Public–private partnerships and a sound innovation ecosystem were key for economic recovery in the Republic of Korea (ROK). The government used the crisis as an opportunity to accelerate digital transformation and provided focused support. The government incentivized corporate social responsibility and ethical corporate behavior as core values and this created a healthy ecosystem within the society. The more prominent the company is, the more social responsibility and corporate ethics the society demands from it.*

With the new norms of wearing masks and social distancing, the ROK has seen daily life and business starting to return to normal and regain vitality amid the pandemic. The Financial Supervisory Service urges banks to keep supporting businesses through extension of loan repayment and deferral of interest repayment.

The Bank of Korea, the central bank of the ROK, increased the limit on loans for financial brokerage assistance by W8 trillion, from W35 trillion to W43 trillion on 24 September 2020 (Bank of Korea 2020). The financial intermediary loans are a system in which the Bank of Korea lends funds to banks at an interest rate of 0.25% to encourage them to extend lending to SMEs. The applied interest rate was cut from 0.75% to 0.25% when increasing the limit of W5 trillion each in February and March (Bank of Korea 2020). Of the recent increase of W8 trillion, W3 trillion is for lending working funds up to W500 million with 1-year maturity for SMEs including self-employed primarily in the service industry. The remaining W2 trillion is for facility fund loans for start-up companies; job creation companies; and materials, parts, and equipment companies (Jang 2020). SMEs and small businesses facing difficulties due to the COVID-19 outbreak are expected to improve financial and liquidity conditions under this scheme. The role of SMEs is critical for helping the economy to recover as SMEs, including micro-businesses and the self-employed, account for 99.9% of 3.5 million registered businesses in in the ROK, and 82.2% of workforce of 14 million people (Park 2020).

### Table 10: Innovative Policy Measures

| Policy/Measures | Organization | Description |
|---|---|---|
| Tech Incubator Program for Startups | Ministry of SMEs and Startups | This program provides research and development funds and mentoring services by matching early-stage startups with large enterprises, angel investors, and venture capitalists. |
| Smart Factory System for SMEs | Ministry of SMEs and Startups and Korea Telecom | Ministry of SMEs and Startups and Korea Telecom established W24 billion of funds together to provide low-interest loans for adopting smart factory to SMEs<br><br>Korea Telecom shares knowledge of its 5G-network-based artificial intelligence technology and smart factor technology with SMEs |
| Good Delivery Application | Local Governments | Local governments develop "good delivery app" without commissions to alleviate small storeowners' financial burden from commissions |
| Social Corporate Responsibility | Baedal Minjok (Korean food delivery company) | The company provides information of New Hope Fund application to restaurant owners through the company's platform |

SMEs = small and medium-sized enterprises.

Source: Adapted from the Ministry of SMEs and Startups and news article http://www.meconomynews.com/news/articleView.html?idxno=45862

The collaborative efforts of the public and private sectors were crucial for the economy to recover. The ROK's economy is expected to decline by 0.8% in 2020, the smallest percentage decrease among OECD forecasts for member nations. Since May, the Ministry of SMEs and Startups has successfully supported the ROK's startup ecosystem through the Tech Incubator Program for Startups (Lee and Lee 2020). The Ministry of SMEs and Startups designates "inclusive companies" such as Samsung Electronics, Hyundai Motor, Kia Motors, Naver and KT matches with early-stage tech startups with innovative ideas, angel investors and venture capitalists, to provide R&D funds and enable startups to focus on advancing their product or services and prepare them when entering the global marketplace. SMEs not only gain financial support but also technological support through networking with private sector partners. For example, the Ministry of SMEs and Startups and KT, a leading mobile carrier in the telecommunications industry, made an agreement to provide W24 billion for more SMEs to adopt the smart factory system, and KT will provide low-interest loans to SMEs through its financial fund on 22 September 2020 (Baek 2020). Also, KT will contribute to the digital innovation by sharing knowledge of its 5G-network-based artificial intelligence technology and smart factory technology. The smart factory refers to a fully integrated technology-based manufacturing system, which connects the entire production process that responds in real-time to meet the changing demands and conditions in the factory, supply network, and customer needs (Wiktorsson et al. 2018). Increasing the company's capacity is essential as the increase of 'untact' (less or no human interaction) demand due to COVID-19 further strengthens the trend of spreading the existing Fourth Industrial Technology business.

**Figure 25: Number of Government-Funded 5G+AI-Based Smart Factories**

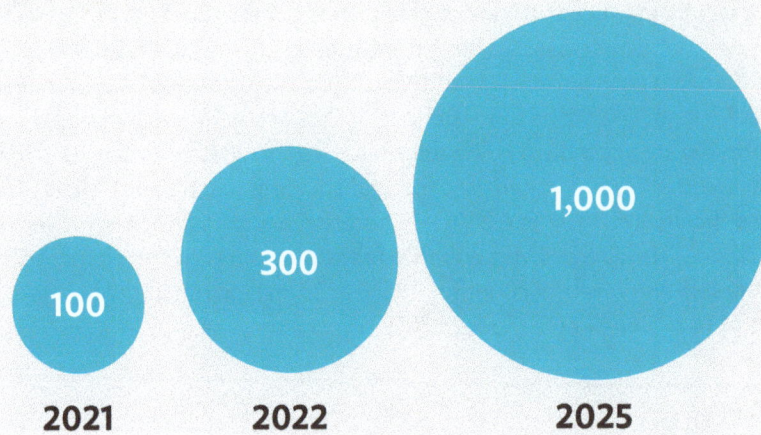

AI = artificial intelligence, SME = small and medium-sized enterprise.
Source: Ministry of SMEs and Startups of the Republic of Korea, 2020

As the digital economy accelerates after COVID-19, the polarization between bio/IT companies and traditional manufacturing companies is expected to intensify, and government initiatives tends to support the bio/IT companies toward digital transformation. The increase in the number of smart factories is expected to bring in innovation to software and hardware industries that deal with robotics, automation equipment, and sensor technologies, manufacturing execution system industries, and 5G service sectors (Lee and Lee 2020). Supporting small enterprises and start-up companies allows them to overcome the crisis more rapidly as their agility and flexibility is superior to medium-sized and large corporations. These companies would turn COVID-19 challenges into business opportunities by flexibly adjusting their business models to a more sustainable and innovative form.

Solutions were provided to help SMEs suffering from poor sales due to COVID-19. In April, Baedal Minjok, the largest food delivery service app operator in the ROK, made changes in commission fees from a monthly flat subscription to a fixed rate charged by the number of delivery cases. The Korea Federation of Micro Enterprise stated that the change would increase the financial burden of small and medium-sized business owners (Park 2020). Local governments decided to develop a "good delivery app" without commissions to protect many storeowners suffering from poor sales and increased financial burden from commissions (Kyeong 2020). Gunsan-si in Jeollabuk-do was the first to develop and launch a public delivery app. Baedal Myeongsu and other local governments such as Gwangjin-gu, Gyeongsangbuk-do region, and Gyeonggi-do region have also launched the public food delivery app. After receiving criticisms from the public for not considering the difficult situation storeowners are facing, Baedal Minjok apologized and decided to improve the pricing system. Also, starting from 29 September, Baedal Minjok used mobile site banners, notification text, and official blog posts to inform the restaurant owners using the platform on how to apply for New Hope Fund for small businesses. Hence, the more prominent the company, the greater the social responsibility and stronger business ethics are demanded.

## Pathways After COVID-19

With government support and private sector effort for mutual growth, economic recovery was possible because of actions of all groups. The next consideration would be which strategy to implement after COVID-19 so that the economy is less vulnerable to such crises in the future.

First, global supply chain strategy after COVID-19 would clearly change in which corporations have to redesign the supply chain to maintain the stability of the supply chain through "design for resilience." Korean manufacturers that relied on foreign suppliers were vulnerable to the pandemic situation. For example, Hyundai Motor, a major automobile manufacturer, had to suspend factory operations in February and shutdown of factories abroad led to shortages of essential parts and materials. Therefore, direct observation and tracking of supply chain through civilization is required for companies to implement a comprehensive supply chain strategy that is agile and flexible in response to global issues (United Nations Development Programme Seoul Policy Centre 2020).

Second, changing the industrial structure would enable a change in the view of sustainable development paradigm in economic fields as the current sustainable development seems to focus mostly on environmental fields such as reducing carbon dioxide emissions. The government's Green New Deal aims to foster economic growth and job creation through investment in the environment. Diversifying markets and promoting trade and overseas investment prepare companies' economic viability in the post COVID-19 era.

Finally, supporting businesses' risk management by identifying and monitoring potential risk factors would be critical for businesses to take preemptive actions against new risks in trade and to strengthen bilateral cooperation with major countries. The government should help businesses with difficulties in international trade because of the entry bans imposed by other countries. Both preemptive and defensive measures should be designed to prepare for changes in society caused by the coronavirus pandemic.

# 4.3  Social Response: Physical (Social) Distancing

*The Republic of Korea's social distancing policy aims to harmonize daily lives and economic activities and prevent COVID-19 infection. In addition, it pursues constant improvement in lifestyle and social structure of the country. Amid the crisis, to secure the quantity of masks quickly and in a stable manner, the government reserved masks as the Public Procurement Service. Thus, mask production and distribution were managed by the government, not the market. Public distributed mask information service allowed people to know where and how many masks were available through a mobile app. Since face-to-face classes became impossible, online schools began to fill the students' learning gaps in public schools. Using the Learning Management System platform, elementary, middle, and high schools nationwide conducted distance learning without opening schools physically. To assist young children and those from less privileged groups, the Ministry of Education provided technical support and consulting. Lastly, the government also provided technical assistance to religious organizations for smartphone-based video recording and transmission of their religious activities. Even technical support for drive-in worship was provided.*

Physical (social) distancing is a public health infectious disease control strategy that minimizes the transmission of infectious diseases by minimizing contact between individuals or groups, and is one of the non-pharmaceutical interventions that are differentiated from intervention strategies using therapeutic agents or vaccines.

COVID-19 is spread primarily by respiratory droplets that directly contact the mucous membranes of the nose, mouth, or eyes. Respiratory droplets are generated during coughing, sneezing, and conversation of an infected person and can be sprayed into the air. These droplets are known to travel limited distances of up to 2 meters.

Thus, limiting contact between people to within 2 meters during the epidemic is effective in preventing infection. Social distancing rules were built based on the basic principles of spreading the disease. In addition, Korean social distancing policies aims to harmonize the daily life and economic activities of the people and prevent infection in preparation for the long-term epidemic.

### Table 11: Main Contents of Each Stage of Social Distancing

| Stage | Stage 1<br>Less than 50 confirmed cases per day/for the Republic of Korea (ROK) | Stage 2<br>More than 50 to less than 100 confirmed cases per day/for ROK | Stage 3<br>More than 100 confirmed cases per day Double the number of confirmed cases twice a week/for ROK |
|---|---|---|---|
| Key message | Comply with quarantine rules and allow daily economic activities | Avoid unnecessary outings, meetings, and use of multi-use facilities | All activities other than essential socioeconomic activities are prohibited in principle |
| Assembly meeting event | Allowed, but recommended to comply with quarantine rules | No more than 50 people indoors and 100 people outdoors | No more than 10 people |
| Sports event | Limit the number of spectators . | No spectators | Stop the game |
| Public-use facilities | Allowed, but some interruptions, restrictions if necessary | Stop operation | Stop operation |
| Private-use facilities | Allow, but refrain from operating high-risk facilities | Suspension of high-risk facilities operation Compulsory compliance with other facility quarantine regulations Limit of number of people per 4 square meters | Suspension of high-risk facilities operation Compulsory compliance with other facility quarantine regulations Shutdown after 9 p.m. |
| School kindergarten day care center | School, or remote classes | School, or remote classes | Remote classes or closed |
| Public institutions· corporations | Minimization of working density through flexible work, or telecommuting (1/3 of all employees) | Minimization of working density through flexible work, or telecommuting (1/2 of all employees) | All employees are recommended to work from home, excluding required personnel |
| Private institutions· enterprises | Recommend activation of flexible work, or telecommuting | Recommend to limit the number of attendees through flexible work, or telecommuting | All employees are recommended to work from home, excluding required personnel |

Source: Adapted from Doctor's News. https://www.doctorsnews.co.kr/news/articleView.html?idxno=135900.

## Supplying Face Masks to Public

As the supply of masks continued to be unable to keep up with the rapidly increasing demand due to the increasing number of COVID-19 confirmed cases, the Government of the ROK implemented the revision of the emergency mask supply and demand adjustment measures on 6 March 2020. The main contents of this measure were the expansion of the mandatory public supply of health masks (currently 50% to 80%) and the suspension of mask exports. In addition, to secure the quantity of masks quickly and in a stable manner, the government unified the contracting entity of public quantity masks as Public Procurement Service (PPS). From this time on, mask production and distribution were managed by the government, not the market. This was implemented as part of the "Emergency supply and demand adjustment measures (If there is a risk of impairing the stability of people's lives due to a sharp rise in inflation or insufficient supply of goods, the government may take emergency supply and demand adjustment measures for goods business owners or import/export companies within a period of 5 months)." in accordance with Article 6 of the Price Stabilization Act, which was the first adjustment measures taken 44 years after the provisions were enacted.

## Guidelines

To stabilize supply and demand for health masks, the government limited the number of masks that can be purchased per person from 9 March 2020 to two per week (three from 27 April). The places where masks can be sold were limited to pharmacies, National Agricultural Cooperative Federation (excluding the capital area), and post offices (located in towns and villages) nationwide. The PPS implemented policy support by granting price incentives to encourage mask manufacturers to increase production. In addition, the Ministry of Defense provided human resources and vehicles for rapid packaging and delivery. The measure was abolished in June as the expansion of mask production facilities increased and the acquisition of raw materials stabilized.

## Implementation

(a)    Publicly Distributed Face Mask Information Service

During the period when the public supply of medical masks was in effect, the government opened the information on the sale of masks to the private sector so that the information (from 10 March 2020) could be quickly used by anyone. Information disclosure was conducted by collecting data related to the purchase and use of masks for each vendor by the Health Insurance Review and Assessment Service and then published online in the National Information Society Agency's public data portal. The data included the name of the mask seller, type of institution, address, date of receipt, inventory, and the date and time data was last created. Using the data provided by the National Information Society Agency, which was reprocessed and released in an open API method, app developers launched services in various forms and provided them to consumers. The above measures were officially abolished in June when the supply and demand for medical masks stabilized, and a special supply and demand management policy was not implemented for simple clothes masks that are not for health use.

**Figure 26: Supply of Face Masks**

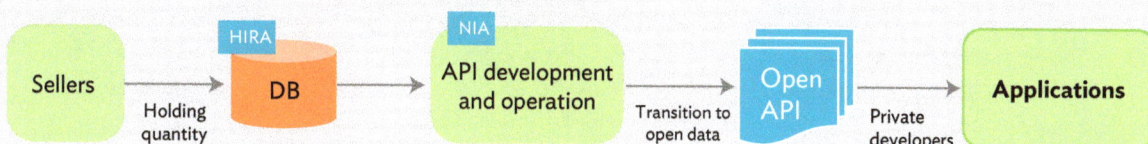

API = application open interface, DB = database.

Source: Modified press release by the Ministry of the Interior and Safety. https://www.mois.go.kr/frt/bbs/type010/commonSelectBoardArticle.do;jsessionid=I5EPNr94XIFfG0s5zx9FtGEF.node50?bbsId=BBSMSTR_000000000008&nttId=76207&bbsTyCode=BBST03&bbsAttrbCode=BBSA03&authFlag=Y&pageIndex=1&searchCnd=&searchWrd=&searchCode1=&searchCode2=&searchCode3=&searchBgnDe=&searchEndDe=&searchSttusCode=.

# Distance Learning: Learning Management System

After the outbreak of COVID-19, the Ministry of Education (MOE) delayed the opening of the new semester of elementary, middle, and high school until 3 April 2020 through three orders of closure. However, as face-to-face classes continued to be difficult within the year, the online school began in earnest from 9 April to prevent students' learning gaps. In preparation for the prolonged closure of business, the MOE strengthened support for distance learning classes and settled them as a regular class method, so that online classes using the LMS platform could be conducted in elementary, middle, and high schools nationwide. In preparation for the prolonged closure of school, the MOE has provided support to conduct online classes using the LMS platform in elementary, middle, and high schools in order to settle the distance class method.

## Guideline

Before implementing distance classes, the MOE distributed notices to schools across the country. For the first and second grades of elementary school, an age where self-directed learning is difficult, the homeroom teacher provided feedback through various methods such as counseling for parents (including wired and wireless) to manage student learning. In addition, educational institutions must adhere to the principle of considering the disadvantaged, such as the disabled and disadvantaged households, to ensure equity in academic rights. Lastly, for teachers who are not familiar with distance learning, the Office of Education and schools provided consulting to improve teachers' ability to design and use online content, while also establishing a support environment such as infrastructure and remote solutions.

## Implementation

Before starting online schooling, the MOE prepared an online learning system using various LMS platforms in cooperation with educational institutions such as the Educational Broadcast System (EBS) and the Korea Education and Research Information Service (KERIS). EBS and KERIS developed the EBS online class and the Cyber e-learning center as platforms, respectively, and, along with the Korean Educational Development Institute, provided educational content on the platform.  However, prior to the COVID-19 epidemic, the educational system in the ROK relied mainly on face-to-face instruction and evaluation, and online learning was an option for individual students other than regular classes. Therefore, students, teachers, and parents were unfamiliar with the sudden, full-scale shift to distance learning classes. For all four readiness measures—technological, contents, pedagogical, and home-based learning support, and monitoring and evaluation readiness—presented by the United Nations Educational, Scientific and Cultural Organization (UNESCO) in preparation for the COVID-19 epidemic (UNESCO, 2020), the ROK needs to be constantly supplemented.

The MOE promoted self-directed learning using autonomous content until the third week of the month through online classrooms, and teacher-managed online learning after the fourth week. On the self-directed learning site, students can select a desired course from the courses provided, register for classes, study lectures, and check their learning history. On the self-directed learning site, students can select and take a course from the courses provided and check their learning history themselves. However, within the LMS, students in online classes take lectures guided by the teacher. The student and the teacher check the learning history together, and the teacher can guide the student's learning. The LMS platforms currently used in the ROK provide learning content and resources, manage the learning process, answer questions, quizzes and tests, discussions, uploading / downloading learning materials, and video lectures.

## Table 12: Learning Management System Platforms Used in the Elementary, Middle, and High School Education Sites

| Platforms | Website | Main Function | Provider |
|---|---|---|---|
| **Cyber e-learning center** | http://cls.edunet.net/ | Provides learning videos and evaluation questions | Ministry of Education |
| **Educational Broadcast System online class** | https://oc.ebssw.kr/ | Attendance, course registration, discussion, assignment submission, and quiz in the online classroom | Educational Broadcast System |
| **Wedorang** | http://rang.edunet.net/ | Attendance, deliver announcements, share materials, and conduct discussions in online classrooms | Ministry of Education |
| **OnSchool** | http://onschool.edunet.net/ | Providing daily learning information, contents (in various fields of culture, art, science), and digital textbooks and a total of 469 e-books. | Ministry of Education |

Source: Author.

## Support for Online Religious Activities

There have been mass infections in several religious establishments, beginning with a large-scale COVID-19 infection in one religious institution in February. Accordingly, the Catholic Archdiocese in the hot spot where the COVID-19 epidemic occurred voluntarily halted face-to-face masses, and many religious groups stressed the need for no-contact religious activities. However, as some small and medium-sized religious facilities complained of technical difficulties, the MSIT implemented temporary support for online religious activities and "drive-in worship" in April 2020.

### Implementation

(a)    Online Religious Activities

MSIT and the Ministry of Culture, Sports and Tourism provided infrastructure and technical assistance to small and medium-sized religious organizations (with fewer than 200 members) that had difficulty conducting online religious activities on their own. The government guided the technical methods for smartphone-based video recording and transmission to religious organizations that applied for support and provided necessary data and communication environment. First, they provided enough data (50 gigabytes data allocation data per month) for video transmission for 2 months from April to May for single line for video transmission for each religious group. Second, they helped build a 5G indoor (in-building) network in religious facilities to improve the quality of the communication network as needed. The government produced and distributed manuals so that religious organizations can easily use internet live video platforms such as Kakao TV and Naver Band Live. In addition, they operated a dedicated call center for technical support and provided on-site support as needed. Accordingly, from 8 April to 29 May 2020, a total of 787 cases were supported, including 536 online broadcasting information support and 216 data support/communication network quality improvement for small and medium-sized religious organizations.

(b)    Drive-In Worship

The government provided technical support for drive-in worship, apart from online religious activities using communication networks. Drive-in worship refers to the transmission of actual religious activities in a limited space such as a parking lot using a small-power radio station, so participants can listen inside their cars and participate in religious activities. MSIT and MSCT have exceptionally allowed the use of radio broadcast frequencies (88 to 108 MHz) for international events in drive-in worship to actively support no-contact religious activities.

**Drive-In Worship.** Members of a Christian church attend an Easter service at a parking lot in southern Seoul, as part of efforts to stem the spread of the new coronavirus. (Photo by Yonhap, Korea Bizwire).

# 5 Points for Discussion

The COVID-19 pandemic management of the Republic of Korea (ROK) has four key features: (i) a strong central autonomous agency that used research for agile and responsive policy making, (ii) public trust in government measures, (iii) strong public–private sector collaboration, and (iv) surveillance and response built on integrated information management systems. The large-scale diagnostic test, which is the basis for quarantine, is based on the fast and highly accurate diagnostic test kit produced through the government's bold R&D investment and technology sharing with developers. Fast and powerful epidemiological investigations were made possible through the establishment of a "smart city" database and information sharing among related ministries. In addition, the government provided various quarantine-related data to the private sector, and the private companies used this data to develop services that reflect the demands of the public, thereby enhancing accessibility.

In addition, there have been many attempts to combine new innovative measures by supplementing the shortcomings of the existing quarantine system in the ROK's response to COVID-19. For example, the drive-through center, which has enabled large-scale diagnostic tests, and the life treatment center, which is a treatment facility for mild patients of COVID-19, were the first to be operated in the country.

Above all, Koreans are cooperative with the government's policies. Koreans who have experienced the influx of infectious diseases from overseas such as the Middle East respiratory syndrome (MERS) have a strong perception that each individual is the quarantine agent. Compared to the pre-COVID-19 epidemic, citizens have higher trust in the central government and civil society, and they practice thorough personal hygiene management, self-diagnosis, and social distancing in their daily lives.

The collection of CCTV images, card usage history, GPS records, and other sources of data to determine the route of the confirmed cases is an important issue for personal information security. According to a recently released United Nations report, both the obligation to protect personal information and the right to know about government measures are stipulated in accordance with domestic related laws, and thus the current quarantine system can be operated in the ROK. However, even if there is public consensus on data collection and trust in the government, the protection of collected personal data must be guaranteed. In particular, as published research indicates that it is possible to re-identify individuals from anonymous data, safe disposal of data collected can be considered the final step in quarantine.

# References

Baek, B. 2020. KT to lead mutual growth with SMEs through smart technology. *Korea Times.* 22 September. https://www.koreatimes.co.kr/www/tech/2020/09/133_296497.html

Bank of Korea. 2020. *Youth-led Innovation & Entrepreneurship for COVID-19: Examples from Republic of Korea.* https://www.undp.org/content/seoul_policy_center/en/home/presscenter/articles/2020/youth-led-innovation---entrepreneurship-for-covid-19--examples-f.html

———. 2020. *Bank of Korea announces 50bp Base Rate cut and measures to stabilize economic and financial conditions.* https://www.bok.or.kr/eng/bbs/E0000634/view.do?nttId=10057026&menuNo=400069

———. 2020. *Bank of Korea provides additional 8 trillion KRW to small business owners and SMEs.*

Central Disease Control Headquarters and Central Disaster Management Headquarters, Republic of Korea. 2020. *Guideline for COVID-19 Response for local governments (Ver 9-2).* http://ncov.mohw.go.kr/duBoardList.do?brdId=2&brdGubun=28

COVID-19 Open API. (n.d.). http://openapi.data.go.kr/openapi/service/rest/Covid19/getCovid19InfStateJson

Cyber learning center. (n.d.). http://cls.edunet.net/

DHL. 2020. *How South Korea juggles cold chain logistics, amid high COVID-19 test kit demand.* https://lot.dhl.com/how-south-korea-juggles-cold-chain-logistics-amid-high-covid-19-test-kit-demand/

EBS online class. (n.d.). https://oc.ebssw.kr/

Government of the Republic of Korea. 2020. *COVID-19, Testing Time for Resilience: In recovering from COVID-19: Korean experience.*

Government of the Republic of Korea. Ministry of Economy and Finance. 2020. *Tackling COVID-19—Health, Quarantine and Economic Measures: Korean Experience.* Ministry of Economy and Finance of Korea: Sejong.

———. 2020. *2nd Supplementary Budget of 2020 Passed.* http://english.moef.go.kr/pc/selectTbPressCenterDtl.do?boardCd=N0001&seq=4895

———. 2020. *3rd Supplementary Budget of 2020 Passed.* http://english.moef.go.kr/popup/20200608_policyFocus/popup.html

————. 2020. *The 3rd Supplementary Budget*. http://english.moef.go.kr/popup/20200608_policyFocus/popup. html

————. 2020. *1st Crisis Management Meeting*. http://english.moef.go.kr/pc/selectTbPressCenterDtl. do?boardCd=N0001&seq=4859

————. 2020. *8th Emergency Economic Council Meeting*. http://english.moef.go.kr/pc/selectTbPressCenterDtl. do?boardCd=N0001&seq=4975

————. (n.d.). *New Deal*. http://www.moef.go.kr/mp/nd/newDeal.do

Government of the Republic of Korea. Ministry of Foreign Affairs. (n.d.). *Korea's Response to COVID-19*. Ministry of Foreign Affairs: Seoul. http://www.mofa.go.kr/eng/index.do

Government of the Republic of Korea. Ministry of Health and Welfare. 2015. A proposition for Infectious Disease Control and Prevention Act, for swift and prompt response to infectious disease, is passed at the Parliament [press release; in Korean]. Ministry of Health and Welfare: Seoul. https://www.mohw.go.kr/react/al/ sal0301vw.jsp?PAR_MENU_ID=04&MENU_ID=0403&CONT_SEQ=323775&page=1

————. 2020.Infectious Disease Control and Prevention Act passed at the Parliament on 4th of August [press release; in Korean]. Ministry of Health and Welfare: Seoul. 4 August. https://www.mohw.go.kr/react/ al/sal0301vw.jsp?PAR_MENU_ID=04&MENU_ID=0403&page=1&CONT_SEQ=358862&SEAR CHKEY=TITLE&SEARCHVALUE=%EA%B0%90%EC%97%BC%EB%B3%91%EC%9D%98+%EC%9 8%88%EB%B0%A9+%EB%B0%8F+%EA%B4%80%EB%A6%AC%EC%97%90+%EA%B4%80%ED- %95%9C+%EB%B2%95%EB%A5%A0

————. 2020. Infectious Disease Control and Prevention Act, Quarantine Act, Medical Service Act passed at the Parliament on 26th of February [press release; in Korean]. Ministry of Health and Welfare: Seoul. 26 February. https://www.mohw.go.kr/react/al/sal0301vw.jsp?PAR_MENU_ID=04&MENU_ ID=0403&page=1&CONT_SEQ=353160&SEARCHKEY=TITLE&SEARCHVALUE=%EA%B0%90%EC%9 7%BC%EB%B3%91%EC%9D%98+%EC%98%88%EB%B0%A9+%EB%B0%8F+%EA%B4%80%EB%A6%A C%EC%97%90+%EA%B4%80%ED%95%9C+%EB%B2%95%EB%A5%A0

————. 2020. Infectious Disease Control and Prevention Act passed at the Parliament on 24th of September [press release; in Korean]. Ministry of Health and Welfare: Korea. 24 September. https://www.mohw. go.kr/react/al/sal0301vw.jsp?PAR_MENU_ID=04&MENU_ID=0403&page=1&CONT_SEQ=36003 3&SEARCHKEY=TITLE&SEARCHVALUE=%EA%B0%90%EC%97%BC%EB%B3%91%EC%9D%98+% EC%98%88%EB%B0%A9+%EB%B0%8F+%EA%B4%80%EB%A6%AC%EC%97%90+%EA%B4%80% ED%95%9C+%EB%B2%95%EB%A5%A0

————. 2020. *COVID 19 in the Republic of Korea*. http://ncov.mohw.go.kr/en

————. 2020. *Operating Guideline for National Safe Hospital*.

————. (n.d.). *COVID-19 Information* [Homepage]. http://ncov.mohw.go.kr/en/

Government of the Republic of Korea. Ministry of Science and ICT. 2020. *How We Fought COVID-19—A Perspective from Science and ICT*.

Gyeonggi Infectious Disease Control Center Homepage. (n.d.). http://www.gidcc.or.kr/

Im, Mina. 2020. Seoul City had the first conference of disaster medical consultative body with 15 hospitals, discussing measures to secure sickbeds [in Korean]. *Yonhap News.* 19 August. https://www.yna.co.kr/view/AKR20200819121100004

Jang, W. 2020. The BOK increases loans for SMEs and small business owners by 8 trillion won. *News.Joins.* 23 September. https://news.joins.com/article/23878952

Kim, S. 2020. BOK to expand financial support for pandemic-hit small merchants. *Yonhap News Agency.* 23 September. https://en.yna.co.kr/view/AEN20200923003600320

Korea Development Institute. 2020. KDI Economic Outlook (September 2020). *KDI Economic Outlook. 37(1).*

Korea Health Industry Development Institute (KHIDI). 2020. COVID-19 Diagnostic Equipment Industry Status and Export Forecast.

Korea Open Access platform for Researchers. (n.d.). https://koar.kr

Korean Government Portal. (n.d.). https://www.gov.kr/portal/main

Korean Society for Laboratory Medicine. (n.d.). http://www.kslm.org/

Korean Society of Infectious Diseases, Korean Society of Pediatric Infectious Diseases, Korean Society of Epidemiology, Korean Society for Antimicrobial Therapy, Korean Society for Healthcare-associated Infection Control and Prevention, and Korea Centers for Disease Control and Prevention. (2020). Report on the epidemiological features of coronavirus disease 2019 (COVID-19) outbreak in the Republic of Korea from 19 January to 2 March 2020. *J Korean Med Sci.* 35e112

Kwon, K. T., J. Ko, H. Shin,M. Sung, and J. Y. Kim. 2020. Drive-Through Screening Center for COVID-19: a Safe and Efficient Screening System against Massive Community Outbreak. *J Korean Med Sci. 35(11).* e123.

Kye, B. and S. Hwang. 2020. Social trust in the midst of pandemic crisis: Implications from COVID-19 of South Korea. *Res Soc Stratif Mobil. 68*

Kyeong, T. 2020. Local Governments Develop Food Delivery App Without Fees. *The Kyunghyang Shinmun.* 7 April. http://english.khan.co.kr/khan_art_view.html?artid=202004072321057

Lee, C and M. Ki. 2015. Strengthening epidemiologic investigation of infectious disease in Korea: lessons from the MERS. *Epidemiol Health. 37*: e2015040.

Lee, D. and E. Lee. 2020. Korean industrial landscape fast turning smart on govt-backed drive. *Pulse News.* https://pulsenews.co.kr/view.php?year=2020

Martin, T. and D. Yoon. 2020. How South Korea Successfully Managed Coronavirus. *The Wall Street Journal.* 25 September. https://www.wsj.com/articles/lessons-from-south-korea-on-how-to-manage-covid-11601044329

National Disaster Safety Portal. (n.d.). https://www.safekorea.go.kr/

National Institute of Medical Device Safety Information (NIDS). 2020. *2020 In Vitro Diagnostic Medical Device Policy Trend Report.* https://www.khidi.or.kr/board/view?pageNum=2&rowCnt=20&no1=1770&linkId=4883 0221&refMenuId=MENU01525&menuId=MENU01521&maxIndex=00488309199998&minIndex=00488 095429998&schType=0&schText=&schStartDate=&schEndDate=&boardStyle=&categoryId=&continent =&country

OECD. 2020. *OECD Economic Outlook, Interim Report.* September 2020. OECD Publishing: Paris. https://doi. org/10.1787/34ffc900-en

OnSchool. (n.d.). from http://onschool.edunet.net/

Park, E. 2020. [Post-COVID-19 New Normal] 'Made in Korea' becomes a must as supply chains collapse. *Korea Joongang Daily.* 13 September. https://koreajoongangdaily.joins.com/2020/09/13/business/industry/ Covid19-supply-chain-GVC/20200913183400407.html

Park, J. and E. Chung. 2020. Learning from Past Pandemic Governance: Early Response and Public-Private Partnerships in Testing of COVID-19 in South Korea. World Development, 105198. DOI: https://doi. org/10.1016/j.worlddev.2020.105198

Park, P. G., C. H. Kim, Y. Heo, T. S. Kim, C. W. Park, and C. Kim. 2020. Out-of-Hospital Cohort Treatment of Coronavirus Disease 2019 Patients with Mild Symptoms in Korea: An Experience from a Single Community Treatment Center. *J Korean Med Sci. 35(13).* e140.

Park, S. 2020. Small business owners criticize food delivery service Baedal Minjok for raising commission. *Aju Daily.* 3 April. https://www.ajudaily.com/view/20200403150926638

Park, S., G. J. Choi, ansd H. Ko. 2020. Information Technology–Based Tracing Strategy in Response to COVID-19 in South Korea—Privacy Controversies. *Jama Network. 323(21).* 2129-2130.

Peck, K. R. 2020. Early diagnosis and rapid isolation: response to COVID-19 outbreak in Korea. *CMI, 26(7).* 805-807.

Rocher, L.,J. M. Hendrickx, and Y. de Montjoy. 2019. Estimating the success of re-identifications in incomplete datasets using generative models. *Nature Communications.* 3069.

Seoul Infectious Disease Control Center Homepage. (n.d.). https://www.scdc.or.kr/

Smart City Korea. (n.d.). https://smartcity.go.kr/

Sohn, J. 2019. Understanding the Task Forces or Foundation to Support Public Health and Medical Services in Metropolitan Governments of South Korea. *Public Health Affair. 3(1).*187-201.

Sung, H., K. H. Roh, K. H. Hong, M. W. Seong,N. Ryoo, and H. S. Kim. 2020. COVID-19 Molecular testing in Korea: practical essentials and answers from experts based on experiences of emergency use authorization assays. *Ann Lab Med. 40.* 439–447.

United Nations. 2020. *Disease pandemics and the freedom of opinion and expression: Human Rights Council forty-fourth session.*

US Food and Drug. 2020. SARS-CoV-2 Reference Panel Comparative Data.

Wedorang. (n.d.). http://rang.edunet.net/

Wiktorsson, M., S. D. Noh, M. Bellgran, and L. Hanson. 2018. Smart Factories: South Korean and Swedish examples on manufacturing settings. *Procedia Manufacturing, 25*, 471-478. doi:10.1016/j.promfg.2018.06.128

## Government Guidelines

*Central Disease Control Headquarters–Central Disaster Management Headquarters.* COVID-19 Response Guideline (for local governments), 9-2 edition. (20.08.20.)

*Central Disease Control Headquarters.*  COVID-19 Quarantine Response Guidelines, 9th Edition. (20.7.9.)

*Central Disease Control Headquarters.* Information for COVID-19 Diagnosis Test (20.2.15)

*KCDC.* COVID-19 medical institution operation case.

*Central Disease Control Headquarters.* COVID-19 Response Guidelines (for medical institutions), 1-1 edition. (2020.8.20)

*Central Disease Control Headquarters.* COVID-19 diagnostic test guideline (for public health institutions), 6th edition. (20.6.26)

*Central Disease Control Headquarters.* Response guidelines of COVID-19 epidemic for collective facilities, multi-use facilities, 2nd edition. (20.2.26.)

*Ministry of Employment and Labor.* Workplace Response Guidelines for Prevention of COVID-19, 8th Edition. (20.4.6.)

*Central Disaster Management Headquarters.* Recommendations for using a face mask to prevent COVID-19

## Applications

(i)     Self-Diagnosis Application. http://ncov.mohw.go.kr/selfcheck/
(ii)    Self-Quarantine Application. http://ncov.mohw.go.kr/shBoardView.do?brdId=2&brdGubun=23&ncvContSeq=1677
(iii)   Emergency Ready App. https://www.mois.go.kr/frt/a02/localGovernmentArticle.do?dicaryinfoid=DICARY_0000000001970
(iv)    Corona Map Application. http://coronamap.site/

www.ingramcontent.com/pod-product-compliance
Lightning Source LLC
Chambersburg PA
CBHW050051220326
41599CB00045B/7369